The Chartered Institute of Management Accountants

CIMA
PUBLISHING

Cost System Design and Profitability Analysis in UK Companies

Colin Drury
Huddersfield University Business School
Mike Tayles
University of Bradford Management Centre

This publication arises from the research project 'Cost Systems Design: A Strategy for Managers – The Product Portfolio' which was funded with a research grant from the CIMA Research Foundation. The award of a Research Foundation grant, and the publication of findings in this format, indicates that the recipient has successfully passed two separate peer review processes, which also involved practitioner assessors. The views expressed in this publication are the authors' own, and do not necessarily represent those of CIMA.

Acknowledgements

The authors are grateful to the reviewers for their helpful comments on earlier drafts of this report.

First published in 2000 by:
The Chartered Institute of Management Accountants
63 Portland Place
London
W1N 4AB

ISBN 1 85971 457 9

Contents

Executive Summary

Introduction

During the last decade most organisations have faced dramatic changes in their business environment. Deregulation, increasing levels in global competition and the emergence of integrated enterprise-wide information systems have provided the impetus for companies to review and redesign their cost systems. Recent theoretical developments in cost system design have also provided a further impetus for organisations to re-examine their cost systems. Much has been written about cost systems throughout the 1990s, and the ideas underpinning activity-based costing have been conceptualised. Little documented evidence exists, however, on the nature and content of cost systems *currently* used within UK companies, the factors influencing the choice of cost system design and the information that is extracted from the cost system for different types of decisions. It is against this background that we approached the Chartered Institute of Management Accountants to fund and sponsor research to examine the above issues. This publication reports the research findings from a postal questionnaire survey undertaken in late 1998 and early 1999. Since many of the issues arising from the recent developments in the literature relating to cost system design are pursued in the research it is important that readers are aware of these developments. Feedback from the survey respondents also indicated a desire for a summary of recent developments within a single publication. The first five chapters of this publication attempt to meet these requirements.

Purposes of cost systems

Cost systems are intended to perform a variety of different functions, including providing decision-making information relating to managing the existing and future mix of activities. This research is primarily concerned with managing the existing mix of activities. The specific objectives of the research are to examine:

- the extent to which different explanatory variables influence the design of cost systems or the information that is extracted;
- the nature, content and role of periodic profitability analysis in managing the existing mix of activities, products, services, locations and customers;
- the treatment of facility-sustaining/infrastructure costs;
- the extent to which companies use a single database for which different costs are extracted for meeting different requirements or the extent to which separate systems are used for generating information for different types of decision;
- the methods used to measure capacity levels to establish denominator levels for calculating cost driver rates;

- the extent to which organisations implement activity-based costing and the purposes for which it is used.

Survey findings

The survey was directed towards larger businesses – those utilising 'developed' cost systems and employing a number of accountants. Annual sales turnover ranged from £25m to over £300m, with most respondents in the larger categories. Replies were received from 187 respondents, giving a response rate of 30 per cent. The survey was directed to both manufacturing and non-manufacturing businesses, and separate information is presented in the report relating to an analysis by different business sectors. More than 90 per cent of the respondents indicated that a single database was maintained from which appropriate cost information was extracted to provide the required information for both inventory valuation and decision-making. Direct costs only were assigned to cost objects by 15 per cent of the responding organisations, and the remaining 85 per cent assigned both direct and indirect costs. Over a typical year the majority of organisations (58 per cent) costed over 200 items within their chosen cost object. Periodic profitability analysis is therefore required to monitor the profitability of activities.

Profitability analysis

Over 90 per cent of the organisations analysed profits at least on an annual basis, and monthly profitability analysis (of products, services, components, customers, locations, etc.) was the norm in approximately 80 per cent of the organisations. Most of the respondents used profitability analysis as an attention-directing mechanism for identifying potential unprofitable activities that required more detailed special studies. Other mechanisms, such as a decline in sales volume or the introduction of a superior product by a competitor, can also signal the need to undertake special studies, but profitability analysis was considered to be the most important.

Of those organisations that assigned indirect costs to cost objects, virtually all of them separately reported short-term incremental costs, and approximately 50 per cent attempted to distinguish between different categories of indirect costs. In particular, they attempted to distinguish between cost assignments using cause-and-effect cost drivers and assignments that do not rely on cause-and-effect allocations. Approximately 80 per cent of the organisations assigned facility-sustaining costs, and the norm was to categorise them separately when extracting information for decision-making. The evidence suggests that most organisations have the potential to use cost information in a flexible manner. Thus, it is possible that criticisms by various commentators relating to the naive use of full costs that incorporate arbitrary cost allocations may have been misleading, because they may have based their criticisms on what is accumulated within the cost system rather than what is reported or extracted from the system for decision-making.

Although most of the organisations trace indirect costs to cost objects, they do not necessarily base their decisions on reported costs that involve indirect cost allocations. Because flexibility exists to extract different categories of costs from the database, it is possible to report a hierarchy of profitability measures within the profitability analysis. The respondents were asked to indicate the most important profitability measures used by their organisations for decision-making. There was approximately a 50/50 split between the use of contribution (sales less direct or variable costs) and a profitability measure that incorporates indirect cost allocations.

Most of the organisations grouped individual products, services or customers together and categorised them as product lines. Approximately 60 per cent of these organisations routinely analysed profits only at the product line level. However, most of the organisations could, if required, extract information from the database to analyse product line profitability at the individual product level. Approximately 20 per cent did not accumulate costs by individual items and therefore could not analyse profitability by individual items within the line.

Details were requested on the information that was used in the special studies. Approximately half of the respondents indicated that an attempt was made to isolate incremental (avoidable) costs when undertaking a detailed appraisal, and the remaining responses indicated that other qualitative factors, or factors that were specific to their organisations, were taken into account. The responses implied that focusing on a profitability measure that included arbitrary allocations of unavoidable costs for attention-directing may not be accompanied by the use of arbitrary allocations within the special studies.

Cost systems

If cost systems fail to capture with sufficient accuracy the resources consumed by cost objects, distorted costs will be reported and there is a danger that potential unprofitable activities will not be highlighted for special studies or that resources will be wasted investigating profitable activities that have been reported as unprofitable within the periodic profitability analysis. Information was collected on the combinations of number of cost drivers and cost pools used by organisations. Many organisations used a large number of cost pools, but only a small proportion of the respondents used a variety of second-stage cost drivers (or allocation bases) to assign indirect costs from cost pools to cost objects. The findings suggest that many organisations are using cost systems that may not accurately assign indirect costs to cost objects. However, it is inappropriate to conclude that organisations have inaccurate cost systems without considering the impact that more sophisticated systems will have on reported costs. It is possible that the observed unsophisticated systems may be reporting costs that are sufficiently accurate for decision-making.

Approximately 25 per cent of the organisations had adopted activity-based costing (ABC), with size and type of business having a significant impact on the adoption rates. The adoption rates were 45 per cent for the largest organisations (annual sales turnover exceeding £300m) and 8 per cent for the smallest organisations (annual sales turnover less than £100m). High adoption rates were observed for financial and service organisations (51 per cent) compared with manufacturing organisations (15 per cent). Although the ABC adopters used significantly more cost pools and cost drivers than the non-adopters, most adopters used fewer cost pools and drivers compared with what is recommended in the literature.

Inventory valuation, pricing and cost driver activity denominator measures

Only 9 per cent of the organisations that assigned costs for inventory valuation purposes used a separate cost accumulation system – one for inventory valuation and the other for decision-making. Virtually all these organisations used a simplistic system for inventory valuation and a more sophisticated system for decision-making. Where the same cost accumulation system was used for inventory valuation and decision-making, the respondents viewed the cost system as being more accurate for inventory valuation, possibly on the grounds that less accurate information is required for inventory valuation.

Cost-plus pricing was used by 60 per cent of the responding organisations as a mechanism to determine selling prices for some of their products or services. It appears that organisations maintain the same cost system for pricing as for decision-making and/or inventory valuation. However, they may extract different information from it. The evidence suggests that some form of full costs, involving indirect cost allocations, was used to a greater extent for cost-plus pricing compared with profitability analysis information that is used for discontinuation, redesign and outsourcing decisions.

It was apparent from the survey that the denominator levels used to establish cost driver rates are not consistent with the recent theoretical approaches that underpin modern cost systems advocated in the literature. Budgeted capacity was used by 90 per cent of the organisations, including ABC adopters, whereas practical capacity is advocated for ABC systems. If practical capacity is not used to establish cost driver rates, then the presumption that modern cost systems represent resource consumption models that distinguish between used and unused resources becomes questionable. Future research should investigate why activity levels different from practical capacity are used. The implications of the use of different capacity levels, for cost systems and the use and provision of information to manage the cost of used and unused capacity, should be explored. Managing the cost of used and unused capacity has been identified as being the central focus of ABC.

Explanatory variables

A major objective of this study was to examine the extent to which potential explanatory variables influenced the sophistication of the observed cost systems and the information that was extracted from the system. Sophistication was generally measured by the extent of the use of different cost pools and cost drivers. Six potential variables were examined: the purposes for which the cost information is required, cost structures, competitive environment, product diversity, size and type of organisation. Because most organisations used a single cost accumulation system, the findings indicated that the purpose for which the information was required did not influence the choice of the cost accumulation system. However, different information appeared to be extracted, depending on the purpose for which the information was required. The findings also suggest that the competitive environment, size and type of business organisation influenced the sophistication of the cost accumulation system. No statistical evidence was found to indicate that product diversity or cost structures were explanatory factors for the sophistication of the cost system. It should be noted, however, that these explanatory variables are notoriously difficult dimensions to capture and measure. Considerable effort was made to obtain this data and this is explained within the report.

Other relationships besides those explicitly defined in the research objectives were examined. There was no evidence to indicate that those organisations that extensively used cost-plus pricing adopted more sophisticated cost systems. The responses for those organisations that adopted direct or variable costing were compared with those that did not in terms of size, cost structures and the number of items costed. There was no significant relationship between these items and the type of cost system adopted.

Focus on managing the mix of existing activities

Finally, it is important to emphasise that this research has concentrated on cost system design and the information generated from the cost system for decisions relating to managing the *existing* mix of activities, products, services, locations and customers. An important related area for future research is to examine the content of management accounting information, and the role it plays, in managing the cost and mix of *future* activities.

1

Introduction

1.1 Background to the study

In the late 1980s a considerable amount of publicity was given to criticisms of product cost measurement and cost systems design. The most notable criticisms were presented in publications by Kaplan (1985, 1988, 1990), Johnson and Kaplan (1987) and Cooper and Kaplan (1988). They claimed that:

- product costs that are computed to meet financial accounting inventory valuation requirements are also used for decision-making;
- over-simplistic allocation methods (such as plant-wide overhead rates) are used to compute product costs and, as a result, distorted product costs are reported;
- direct labour-based overhead rates are extensively used, despite labour costs declining in importance, and being an inappropriate cost driver for many overhead costs;
- external financial reporting conventions encourage a financial accounting mentality and this has resulted in product costing practices following, and becoming subservient to, financial accounting practices.

The above criticisms were derived mainly from observations in the USA. They were also derived from studies of a small number of companies, or informal contacts between academics and practitioners, and not from large-scale surveys of practice. For example, Anthony (1989, p.18) stated: 'Information about management accounting practices is abysmally poor' and 'Almost all information is anecdotal.' He argued that there is a need for survey information relating to the use of management accounting techniques, and criticised the assumptions that are often made in the literature that a particular technique is used by most companies when no statistical evidence is available relating to how many companies use that technique. These views were also reinforced by Holzer and Norreklit (1991, p.7) who stated: 'Cost accounting practices in industry are difficult to verify since no reliable survey data is available.'

During the early 1990s surveys of management accounting practices were undertaken in many countries. These surveys provided a useful overview of current practices and techniques that are used. Although product costing case study research has been undertaken, most of this has focused on activity-based costing (ABC).

Besides studying product costing practice, considerable attention has also been given to product costing theory. During the 1980s the limitations of traditional product cost systems and the superiority of ABC systems were widely publicised. ABC, however, is not a recent innovation. Fifty years ago Goetz (1949) advocated ABC principles when he wrote:

> Each primary [overhead] class should be homogeneous with respect to every significant dimension of management problems of planning and control. Some of the major dimensions along which [overhead] may vary are number of units of output, number of orders, number of operations, capacity of plant, number of catalogue items offered.... (p.142)

Decreasing information processing costs resulted in a few firms in the USA and Europe implementing ABC-type systems during the early 1980s. In a series of articles based on observations of innovative ABC-type systems Cooper and Kaplan conceptualised the ideas underpinning these systems and coined the term ABC. These articles were first published in 1988. They generated a considerable amount of publicity and consultants began to market and implement ABC systems before the end of the decade. In a survey of UK companies, Innes and Mitchell (1991) reported that approximately 10 per cent of the surveyed companies had implemented, or were in the process of implementing, ABC. Based on their experience of working with early US adopters, Cooper and Kaplan articulated their ideas and reported further theoretical advances in articles published between 1990 and 1992. ABC ideas have now become firmly embedded in the management accounting literature and educational courses, and many practitioners have attended conferences on the topic.

During the last decade most organisations have also faced dramatic changes in their business environment. Deregulation, increasing levels in global competition, the reduction in information processing costs, the emergence of integrated enterprise-wide information systems available from software companies like SAP and Oracle, and the publicity given to theoretical developments in product costing have provided the impetus for companies to review and redesign their product cost systems. Little documented evidence exists, however, on the nature and content of product cost systems *currently* used within UK companies, the factors influencing the choice of cost system design and the information that is extracted from the cost system for different types of decision. It is against this background that we approached the Chartered Institute of Management Accountants to fund and sponsor research to undertake a postal questionnaire survey to examine the above issues.

1.2 Outline of the report

This report consists of 10 chapters. The second chapter focuses on cost system design issues. In particular, the functions of a cost system, the different levels of accuracy required for the different functions, and the problems in identifying and extracting relevant cost information for decision-making are discussed. Much has been written about product costing throughout the 1990s, and the ideas underpinning ABC have been conceptualised. Since many of the issues arising from this literature are pursued in the survey, it is important that readers are aware of the recent developments. Also, our discussions with the survey respondents indicated a demand for a summary of the recent developments within a single publication. Chapter 3 aims to meet these requirements. In Chapter 4, previous research relating to the issues pursued in this study is summarised. This is followed by a chapter which identifies and discusses the impact of potential explanatory variables which may influence the design of a cost system and the information that is reported.

The final five chapters concentrate on the empirical study. Chapter 6 provides an overview of the study and identifies and discusses the objectives of the research. The survey findings are presented in Chapters 7–9. In Chapter 7, the findings relating to the cost information that is accumulated and extracted for periodic profitability analysis are presented. Areas investigated include the role of periodic profitability analysis, cost information incorporated within the profitability analysis, the importance of alternative profitability measures, the content of special studies, and details relating to the cost systems used to support profitability analysis. Chapter 8 focuses on cost information for stock valuation and pricing decisions and also on the activity levels that are used for cost assignment. In Chapter 9, the findings relating to the extent to which the potential explanatory variables described in Chapter 5 influence the observed cost systems and the information that is extracted are presented. A brief conclusion to the study is provided in Chapter 10.

2

Cost System Design Issues

2.1 Functions of a cost system

Companies need cost systems to perform a number of different functions. They include:

- allocating costs between cost of goods sold and inventories for internal and external profit reporting;
- providing relevant cost information to manage the cost and mix of existing activities, products, services, locations and customers;
- providing economic feedback to managers to manage costs and improve the efficiency and effectiveness of existing operations;
- providing relevant information to manage the cost and mix of future activities.

The first three functions relate to generating information relating to existing activities. Stock valuation is not an issue for many non-manufacturing organisations, and these organisations therefore do not require a cost system to perform the first function. The second function is concerned with ensuring that only profitable activities are undertaken. The cost system plays a crucial role here in generating information for periodic profitability analysis for distinguishing between profitable and unprofitable activities. When unprofitable activities are identified, cost reduction alternatives, such as outsourcing or redesign, are considered. If cost reduction or actions taken to generate additional revenues cannot make these activities profitable, and there are no other strategic reasons (such as maintaining a full product line) for continuing the activities, they are likely to be subjected to discontinuation. In some situations cost information extracted from the cost system also plays a crucial role in determining selling prices. For example, product costs may be of vital importance in determining selling prices, particularly in thin markets where customised products are provided that do not have readily available market prices. The third function relates to operational cost control and includes traditional responsibility accounting, standard costing and variance analysis.

Whereas the first three functions are essentially feedback-oriented, the fourth function relies on feedforward techniques. Here the focus is on managing future activities to ensure that only profitable products and services are launched. The existing costing database is unlikely to be appropriate for this function. Instead, the emphasis is on providing estimates of future cost information using techniques such as target costing, life-cycle costing and value engineering.

It is not feasible to investigate all of the above four functions within a single survey. The major objective of this research project is to focus on the second function: in particular, cost system design and the information generated from the cost system for decisions relating to managing the existing mix of activities, products, services, locations and customers. However, given that previous research suggests that the same cost information is used for both stock valuation and decision-making, the research will also incorporate cost systems used for stock valuation in order to examine how they interrelate with cost information accumulated and generated for decision-making.

2.2 Different accuracy requirements

The accuracy of the reported costs should be dependent upon the purpose for which the cost information is required. In order to meet financial accounting requirements it may not be necessary to measure accurately the resources consumed by *individual* products. A well-designed product cost system should analyse accurately the *total* cost incurred during a period between cost of sales and inventories.

For decision-making purposes, more accurate product costs are needed to distinguish between profitable and unprofitable products and activities. If the cost system does not capture accurately enough the consumption of resources by products, the reported product costs will be distorted, and there is a danger that managers may drop profitable products or continue the production of unprofitable products. Where product costs are used to determine selling prices, the undercosting of products can result in the acceptance of unprofitable business, whereas overcosting can result in bids being rejected and the loss of profitable business.

Kaplan and Cooper (1998, p. 22) advocate that, because of the different levels of accuracy that are required, manufacturing companies should use two separate product cost systems, one for decision-making and the other for inventory valuation. They argue that most organisations use a single traditional cost system, designed primarily to meet financial accounting inventory requirements, to generate cost information for decision-making requirements. Such costs are accurate enough for financial accounting, but are mostly totally inadequate in terms of accuracy for decision-making.

Because existing systems remain adequate for financial accounting Kaplan and Cooper (1998, p. 22) recommend that companies maintain and use their existing database for preparing external financial accounts and, separate from their official financial accounting database, develop customised, stand-alone approaches (using activity-based costs) for decision-making. The stand-alone ABC database can be maintained at standard cost which should be periodically reviewed, say, once or twice a year. After having fully tested stand-alone ABC systems and truly understood their capabilities and limitations, they suggest that companies should develop fully integrated activity-based systems that provide a single database from which different costs can be extracted for different purposes. Expenses assigned to individual products but which should not be allocated for inventory valuation will be stripped away. For decision-making, only those costs that are relevant to the decision will be extracted from the database.

2.3 Identifying cost information that is relevant for decision-making

For meeting stock valuation requirements, external reporting requirements specify the costs that should be assigned to products. In most countries, direct manufacturing costs plus a share of indirect manufacturing costs are assigned to products for stock valuation. Non-manufacturing costs are treated as period costs and are not assigned to products.

For decision-making, conventional wisdom, as portrayed in textbooks and reflected in management accounting education, advocates that incremental costs that predict future cash flows arising from decisions should be used. Such costs are also described as decision-relevant costs, avoidable costs, marginal costs, attributable costs and, when they are deducted from incremental revenues, the term 'contribution' is often used. There is generally common agreement that decisions should be based on the incremental costs arising from a decision. However, disagreement arises as to how incremental costs should be measured. Until recently most textbooks have had a tendency to adopt a short-term perspective when illustrating decision-relevant costs, which has meant that fixed costs have been assumed to remain constant whatever future decisions were taken. Therefore, variable costs represented the only incremental costs that were relevant for making short-term decisions if capacity constraints did not apply. For alternatives requiring the use of scarce capacity, incremental costs represent the sum of variable costs and the opportunity cost arising from the use of the scarce capacity. Where a longer-term perspective is adopted, capacity constraints can be removed and incremental costs consist of variable costs plus those fixed costs that could be avoided if a product was discontinued. What constitutes incremental cost is therefore dependent on the time horizon under consideration.

Conventional wisdom thus appears to provide a mechanism for extracting the costs that should be used for both short-term and long-term decisions. Product profitability should be periodically reviewed, adopting both a short-term and an appropriate long-term time horizon. With a long-term perspective each product's incremental revenues should be compared with its long-term incremental costs. Such costs should be derived from assigning variable costs plus those fixed costs that would be avoidable if the product was dropped. This approach is fine for the highly simplified situations assumed in textbooks where it is typically assumed that an organisation markets only three or four products. All that needs to be done is to undertake special studies for each product to extract the uniquely avoidable costs that would arise from discontinuation.

If we move from simplified textbook situations to the real world, where most organisations have hundreds of products or services, conventional wisdom can still capture incremental/avoidable costs provided that all the incremental costs arising from a decision relating to a single product are uniquely attributable to that product. In this situation direct incremental/avoidable costs can be easily extracted from the cost system. However, not all incremental fixed costs are direct costs uniquely attributable to a product. Some indirect costs are also incremental in the longer term. Such costs include a share of the cost of those joint resources that fluctuate in the longer term according to the demand for them. Most costs falling within this category are support department costs. For example, if a product consumes 10 per cent of the resources of the purchasing activity, and in the long term the costs of the resources fluctuate according to the demand for them, then if the product under review is dropped, 10 per cent of purchasing costs would be avoidable. Such indirect costs are difficult to capture applying the decision-relevant approach advocated by conventional wisdom.

A further problem relating to those joint resources that fluctuate in the long term according to the demand for them is that, if we focus on individual products, the incremental/avoidable costs arising from a decision to add or drop a single product/service may be zero. Assuming that 20 products are viewed in this manner, then the sum of the incremental costs will be zero. However, if the 20 products are viewed as a whole there may be a significant change in resource usage and incremental costs. A similar view was expressed by one of the respondents participating in the research project. He stated: 'If we close down one branch then branch support costs will not change but if we close down 20 branches significant changes will be made.'

Cooper (1990a) also argues that decisions should not be viewed independently. He states:

> The decision to drop one product will typically not change 'fixed' overhead spending. In contrast, dropping 50 products might allow considerable changes to be made. Stated somewhat tritely, the sum of the parts (the decision to drop individual products) is not equal to the sum of the whole (the realisable savings from having dropped 50 products). To help them make effective decisions, managers require cost systems that provide insights into the whole, not just isolated individual parts. (p. 58)

In order to apply conventional wisdom to estimate the avoidable costs arising from changes in those joint resources that fluctuate according to the demand for them, it is necessary to undertake special studies for each product, or combination of products, for which a decision is required. This approach is only feasible for organisations that market a small number of products or services. For those organisations that have more than a few products, the range of potential decisions to explore undertaking special studies is enormous and unmanageable. For example, a company with only 100 products has a potential of $2^{100}-1$ product mix decisions. To cope with this situation, organisations need attention-directing information to highlight those specific activities, or combination of activities, that appear to be questionable and which require further detailed special studies to ascertain their viability. Periodic profitability analysis meets this requirement. A cost accumulation system is therefore required to periodically assign costs to cost objects for routine periodic profitability analysis.[1]

---

1 We define a cost object as any activity, product/service, location or customer for which a separate measurement of cost is required. For simplicity of presentation within the report, it is sometimes assumed that products are the cost objects. However, alternative cost objects can be substituted for the term 'product'.

2.4 Types of cost system

Cost systems can vary in terms of what costs are assigned to cost objects and their level of sophistication. Traditionally, cost systems have been classified for inventory valuation purposes, but here we are concerned with cost systems for routine profit reporting for providing attention-directing information for decision-making. Typically, cost systems are classified as follows:

- variable cost systems;
- direct cost systems;
- traditional absorption cost systems;
- activity-based cost systems.

Variable cost systems assign only variable costs to cost objects, and the difference between sales revenues and variable costs is defined as contribution to *fixed costs* and profit. With variable cost systems, activities that have negative or low contributions to fixed costs are highlighted for special studies, and fixed costs can be taken into account at this stage. Variable costs are interpreted as consisting of only short-term variable costs (normally direct materials and direct labour within manufacturing organisations). The disadvantage of this method is that avoidable fixed costs are not assigned to cost objects.

Direct cost systems only assign direct costs to cost objects. The difference between sales revenues and direct costs represents the contribution to *indirect* costs and profit. They are appropriate where the cost of those joint resources that fluctuate according to the demand for them is insignificant. Using direct cost systems requires that activities that have negative or low contributions to indirect costs are highlighted for special studies. An estimate of those indirect costs that are relevant to the decision should then be incorporated within the special studies. Thus, indirect costs are not accumulated or reported within the routine reporting system. The focus is on contribution to indirect costs for routine reporting and as an attention-directing device. However, an attempt is made to incorporate indirect costs within a more detailed analysis if special studies are undertaken. In contrast, both traditional and ABC systems assign indirect costs to cost objects. The major features of these systems are reviewed in the next chapter.

3

Summary of Recent Product-costing Literature

3.1 Comparison of traditional and ABC systems

This chapter identifies the distinguishing features of traditional and ABC systems and briefly describes some of the recent theoretical advances in ABC systems. Figure 3.1 provides an overview of both systems for manufacturing organisations. Both use a two-stage allocation process. In the *first stage* a traditional system allocates overheads (i.e. indirect costs) to production and service departments and then reallocates the service department costs to the production departments. Within this first stage, two approaches are used to assign indirect costs to production and service departments. Some costs (e.g. supervision) can be directly attributed to departments, whereas others, such as lighting and heating, are apportioned using allocation bases (e.g. floor area) to estimate the departmental usage of common resources that are jointly used by departments. Service department costs are reallocated to production departments using allocation bases that attempt to measure the benefits that the production departments receive for the services rendered.

In contrast, an ABC system assigns indirect costs to each major activity (rather than departments), but the procedure is virtually the same as that used for traditional systems. With ABC systems many activity-based cost centres (alternatively known as cost pools) are established, whereas with traditional systems indirect costs tend to be pooled by departments, although they are normally described as cost centres.

Activities consist of the aggregation of many different tasks and are described by verbs associated with objects. Typical support activities include schedule production, set up machines, move materials, purchase materials, inspect items, process supplier records. Production process activities include machine products and assemble products. Thus within the production process, activity cost centres are often identical to the cost centres used by traditional cost systems. Support activities are also sometimes identical to cost centres, such as when the purchasing department and activity are both treated as cost centres. Overall, however, ABC systems will normally have a greater number of cost centres.

The *second stage* of the two-stage allocation process allocates costs from cost pools to products or other chosen cost objects. Traditional cost systems trace indirect costs to products using a small number of second-stage cost drivers, which vary directly with the volume produced. Instead of using the term 'cost driver' the terms 'allocation bases', 'absorption bases' and 'overhead allocation rates' tend to be used, and the process is often described as indirect costs being absorbed by products or services. Direct labour hours, machine hours and sometimes direct material cost are the volume bases that are normally used by traditional cost systems. In contrast, ABC systems use many different second-stage cost drivers, including non-product-volume-based drivers, such as number of production runs for production scheduling and the number of purchase orders for the purchasing activity. A further distinguishing feature is that traditional systems normally assign service/support costs within the production department cost driver rates, whereas ABC systems tend to establish separate cost driver rates for assigning the cost of support activities to cost objects.

Therefore the major distinguishing features of ABC systems are that they:

- tend to rely on a greater number of cost centres and are based on activities rather than departments;
- use a greater number, and also a more diverse range, of second-stage cost drivers.

By using a greater number of cost centres and a more diverse range of cost drivers that cause activity resource consumption, and assigning activity costs to cost objects on the basis of cost driver usage, ABC systems can more accurately measure the resources consumed by cost objects. Traditional cost systems report less accurate cost because they use cost drivers where no cause-and-effect relationships exist to assign support costs to cost objects.

Figure 3.1 The two-stage allocation process for traditional and activity-based cost systems

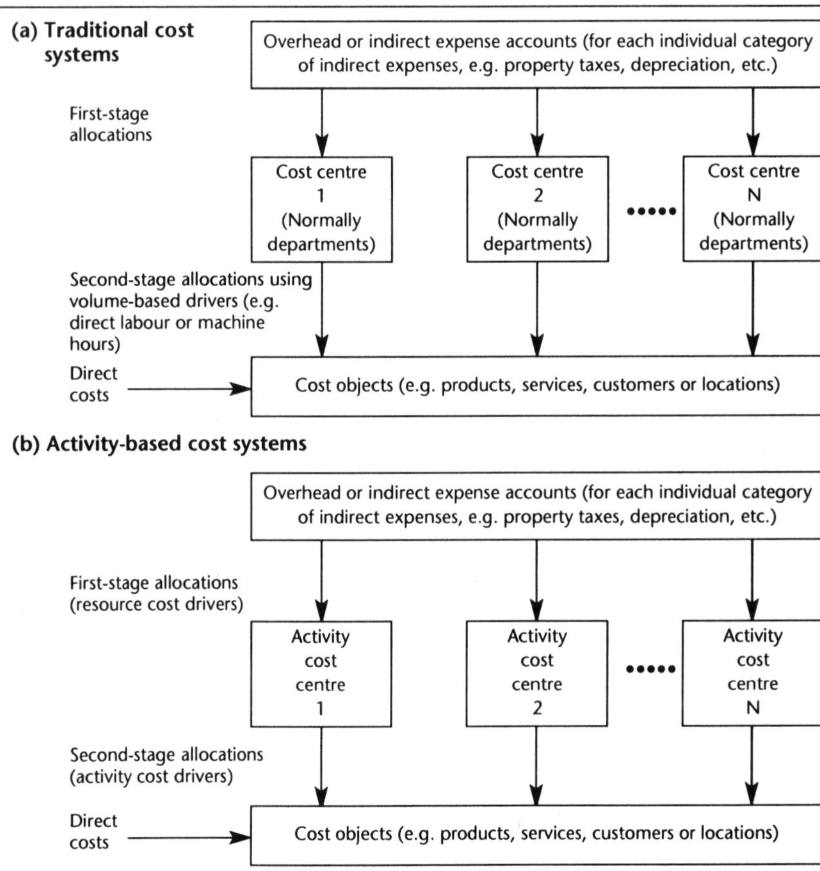

3.2 Hierarchy of activities

During the 1990s ABC theory was refined. Some commentators initially exaggerated the benefits of early ABC systems. These exaggerated claims resulted in criticisms of ABC theory, particularly from academics. The theoretical developments thus emerged as a response to the criticisms of early ABC systems.

The first theoretical development was reported by Cooper (1990b, p. 6), describing a hierarchy of activities (unit, batch, product-sustaining and facility-sustaining). Unit-level activities are performed each time a unit of the product or service is produced. Expenses in this category include direct labour, direct materials, energy costs and machine maintenance. Unit-level activities consume resources in proportion to the number of units of production and sales volume. Typical cost drivers for unit-level activities include labour hours, machine hours and the quantity of materials processed. These cost drivers are also used by traditional cost systems. Traditional systems are therefore also appropriate for assigning the costs of unit-level activities to cost objects.

Batch-level activities include setting up a machine for a production run, purchasing materials and processing a customer's order. For a manufacturing organisation they are performed each time a batch of goods is produced. The resources required to perform a batch-level activity vary with the number of batches made and are independent of the number of units in the batch. In other words, the same quantity of resources are required to set up a machine to produce 10 or 5,000 items. Traditional cost systems mostly treat the expenses of performing batch-level activities as fixed, although they are sometimes incorporated within volume-based variable overhead rates.

Product-sustaining activities are performed to enable the production of individual products (or services) to occur. The resources consumed by these activities are independent of the output and mix of the products (or services) sold. Examples of product-sustaining activities provided by Kaplan and Cooper (1998, p. 90) include maintaining and updating product specifications and technical support provided for individual products and services. Kaplan and Cooper also extend the notion of product-sustaining beyond manufacturing to incorporate customer-sustaining activities, which represent work that enables a company to sell to an individual customer that is also independent of the volume or mix of the products/services sold. Customer market research and support fall within this activity category.

The final activity category identified by Cooper (1990b) is facility-sustaining activities. They are performed to sustain a facility's general manufacturing process and include administration staff, plant management and plant property costs. They are common and joint to all products manufactured within the facility and are therefore not assigned to individual products. More recently, Kaplan and Cooper (1998, p. 259) have incorporated other activity categories that should not be traced to individual products or customers. They include brand or product line sustaining activities that support an entire brand or product line (e.g. product development and advertising), and channel-sustaining activities, such as advertising. The expenses associated with these activities should be assigned directly to the individual product lines, facilities and channels, but they should not be allocated down to the individual products, services or customers within these categories.

In developing an ABC cost hierarchy, Kaplan and Cooper (1998, pp. 260–3) have sought to assign all organisational expenses to a particular hierarchical or organisational level where cause and effect can be established. In an ABC system they state that every cost assignment to an activity or cost object should be transparent and traceable, via cause-and-effect relationships, to the demand for the resources by the cost object. Arbitrary allocations should be avoided, since no cause-and-effect relationship can be established. Thus the ABC model described in Figure 3.1 does not attempt to assign all costs (e.g. facility, product and brand-sustaining costs) through cost centres to individual products or services marketed by an organisation.

3.3 Profitability analysis and attention-directing information

The second theoretical development was first highlighted by Kaplan (1990, p. 14) and Cooper and Kaplan (1991, p. 278). They stress that reported product costs do not provide information that can be used directly for decision-making. Instead, they report attention-directing information by highlighting those products or services that require more detailed special studies. Cooper (1997, p. 17) has stressed that a major role of ABC is to develop profitability maps (i.e. periodic profitability analysis by cost objects) that are used to focus managerial attention. He argues that because the cost of special studies is high, the number performed has to be carefully controlled; hence the need for good attention-directing information. He concludes that the primary value of activity-based systems lies in the quality of the profitability analysis generated. Their greater accuracy increases the probability that when the special study is undertaken, its findings will support the message sent by the cost system. In other words, profitable products will be found to be profitable, and unprofitable products will be found to be unprofitable. Traditional cost systems often result in inaccurate profitability analysis, resulting in special studies being at odds with the message sent by the cost system. In the extreme, the cost system may be ignored.

Kaplan and Cooper (1998, pp. 261–3) incorporate cost hierarchies to develop activity-profitability maps by cost objects. The general principles of activity-profitability maps (or profitability analysis) analysed by cost objects is illustrated in Figure 3.2. This approach categorises costs according to the causes of their variability at different hierarchical levels. Hierarchies identify the lowest level to which cost can meaningfully be assigned without relying on arbitrary allocations. In Figure 3.2, the lowest hierarchical levels (shown at the top of the diagram) are product, customer and branch contributions and the highest levels (shown at the bottom of the diagram) are product lines, distribution channels and country profits. The hierarchical approach helps to identify the impact on resource consumption by adding or dropping items at each level of the hierarchy. For example, Kaplan and Cooper point out that, if a brand is dropped, activities at the brand level and below (i.e. above the brand profits row in Figure 3.2) will be affected, but higher-level activities (i.e. at the product line level) will be unaffected. Similarly, if a product within a particular brand is dropped, then all unit, batch and product-sustaining costs uniquely associated with that product will disappear.

Figure 3.2 Hierarchical profitability analysis

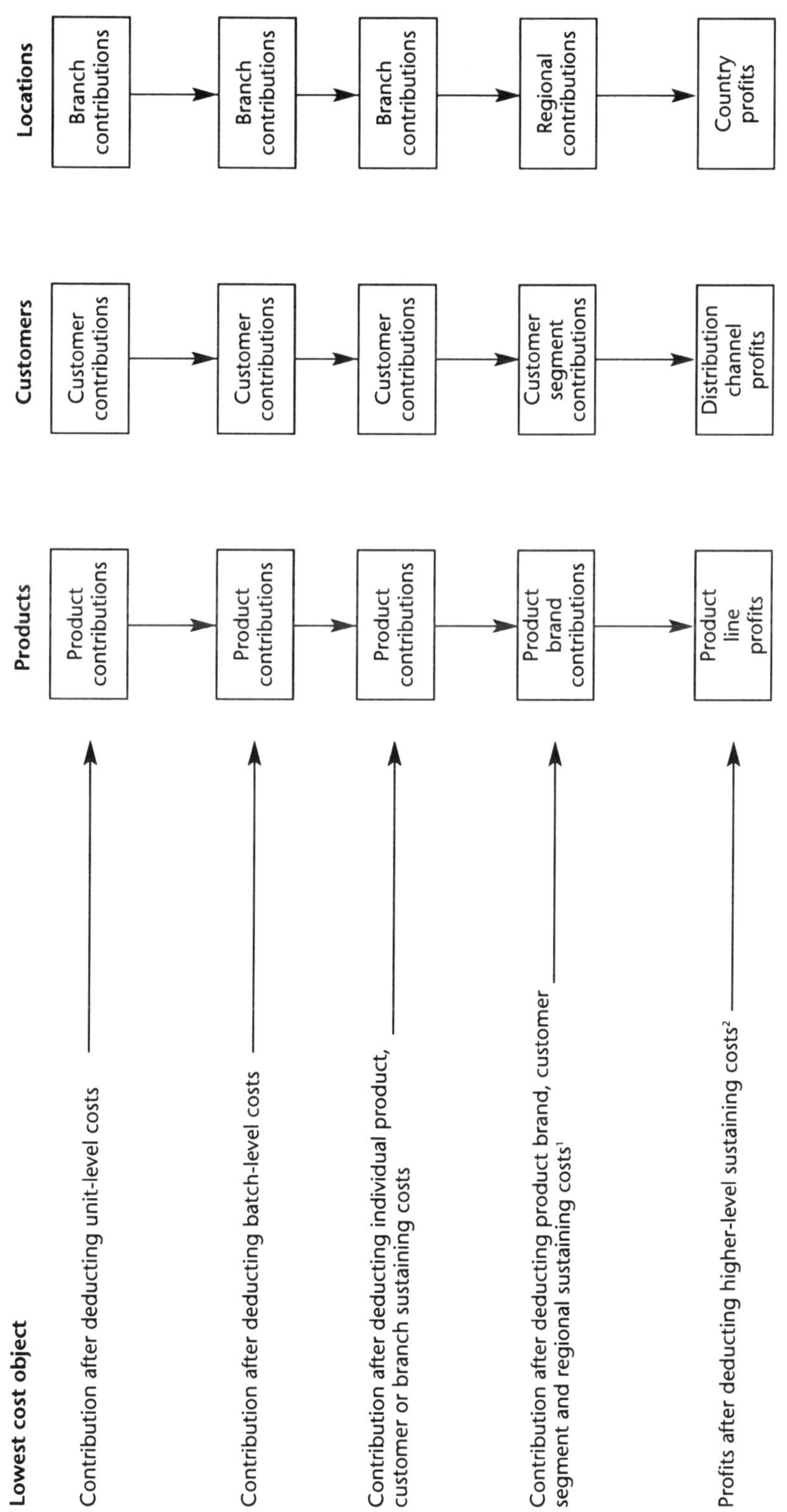

Notes

[1] Consists of expenses dedicated to sustaining specific product brands or customer segments or regions, but which cannot be attributed to individual products, customers or branches.

[2] Consists of expenses dedicated to sustaining the product lines or distribution channels or countries, but which cannot be attributed to lower items within the hierarchy.

3.4 Resource consumption models

The third, and possibly the most important, theoretical advance in ABC systems was reported by Cooper and Kaplan (1992) in a paper which emphasised that ABC systems are models of resource consumption. The paper showed how ABC systems measure the cost of using resources and not the cost of supplying resources, and highlighted the critical role played by unused capacity. Kaplan (1994) used the following equation to formalise the relationship between activity resources supplied and activity resources used for each activity:

$$\text{Cost of resources supplied} = \text{Cost of resources used} + \text{Cost of unused capacity} \quad (3.1)$$

The left-hand side of the equation indicates that the amount of expenditure on an activity depends on the cost of resources supplied rather than the cost of resources used. Periodic financial accounting statements measure the expenses incurred to make resources available (i.e. the cost of resources supplied), whereas ABC systems measure the cost of resources used for individual products, services or customers.

The difference between the cost of activity resources supplied and the cost of resources used represents the cost of unused capacity. Unused capacity arises because the supply of some resources has to be acquired in discrete amounts in advance of usage such that the supply cannot be continually adjusted in the short run to match exactly the usage of resources. Typical expenses in this category include the acquisition of equipment or the employment of non-piecework employees. The expenses of supplying these resources are incurred independently of usage in the short run and this independence has led to them being categorised as fixed costs, although Kaplan and Cooper (1998, p. 120) describe such resources as 'committed resources'. In contrast, there are other types of resource whose supply can be continually adjusted to match exactly the usage of resources. For example, materials, casual labour and the supply of energy for running machinery can be continually adjusted to match the exact demand. Thus the cost of supplying these resources will generally equal the cost of resources used and the resources will have no unused capacity. Kaplan and Cooper (1998, p. 121) classify these resources as 'flexible resources', although they have traditionally been categorised as variable costs.

Managers make decisions (e.g. changes in output volume and mix, process changes and improvements and changes in product and process design) that result in changes in activity resource usage. Assuming that such decisions result in a decline in the demand for activity resources, then the first term on the right-hand side of equation (3.1) will decline (the cost of resources used), but the cost of unused capacity (the second term on the right-hand side of the equation) will increase to offset exactly the lower resource usage cost. To translate the benefits of reduced activity demands into cash-flow savings, management must remove the unused capacity from the system by reducing spending on the supply of the resources. Thus to make a resource variable in the downward direction requires two management decisions – first to reduce the demand for the resource and, second, to lower the spending on the resource.

Demands for activity resources can also increase because of decisions to introduce new products, expand output and create greater product variety. Such decisions can lead to situations where the demand for activity resource usage exceeds the supply of resources, thus requiring a decision to increase the spending on the supply of resources.

A major feature of ABC systems is therefore that reported product, service or customer costs represent estimates of the cost of resources used. In the case of flexible resources, cash-flow changes will soon follow decisions to reduce activity usage, such as dropping a product, but for committed resources performing one less set-up, ordering one less batch of materials or undertaking one fewer engineering change notice will not result in an automatic reduction in spending. It will create additional capacity, and changes in spending on the supply of resources will often be the outcome of the totality of many decisions rather than focusing on a one-off product decision. Such ideas are considered to be of such vital importance by Kaplan and Cooper (1998, p. 122) that they conclude that managing used and unused capacity is 'the central focus of ABC'.

3.5 Capacity levels for establishing cost driver rates

In order to measure the cost of used and unused capacity it is necessary to use practical capacity as the denominator level for determining the activity cost driver rates. The following illustration adapted from Kaplan and Cooper (1998, p. 122) illustrates the approach. Assume that for the purchasing activity the budgeted expenses for the next period are £300,000 and that the maximum number of purchase orders that can be processed during the period is 15,000 (i.e. the practical capacity), then the estimated cost of processing each purchase order is £20. If the budgeted level of usage for the cost driver is 14,000 orders, then the budgeted cost of unused capacity will be £20,000 (1,000 orders at £20), and if the actual level of usage is only 12,000 the unplanned cost of unused capacity will be £40,000. Therefore the total cost of unused capacity is £60,000, consisting of £20,000 planned and £40,000 unplanned.

If activity cost driver rates are computed on a historical basis, then 12,000 orders will be used as the denominator level and the cost driver rate will consist of the sum of the cost of resource usage and the cost of resources that were not used. Therefore the cost of used and unused capacity cannot be separately reported. Alternatively, if the budgeted usage of 14,000 orders is used, the cost driver rate will incorporate the cost of the planned unused capacity and only the unplanned cost of unused capacity will be reported. Budgeted activity usage is only appropriate if a company uses activity-based budgeting and eliminates unused capacity prior to the budget period by reducing spending on the supply of resources to match the practical capacity supplied with the planned usage.

In the above illustration, practical capacity was measured in terms of human resources. It is much easier to measure practical capacity for human rather than physical resources. This is because such resources tend to be flexible in the longer term. It is therefore realistic to plan to adjust practical capacity supplied for the activity to the planned demand for activity resources. However, physical resources, such as physical asset acquisitions, are less flexible and often can only be supplied in large increments. For example, maximum demand for a machine might only be 80 per cent of its practical maximum capacity. If the next smaller version of the machine has a capacity of only 60 per cent of the larger machine, the company will acquire the larger machine. In these circumstances Kaplan and Cooper (1998, p. 128) suggest that if the machine was purchased in the full knowledge that the maximum utilisation would be 80 per cent of its potential maximum capacity, then the denominator level that should be used for measuring cost driver practical capacity is the 80 per cent level.

3.6 Cost versus benefits considerations

If organisations choose to assign to cost objects a share of the cost of those resources that fluctuate in the long term according to the demand for them, but which are not uniquely attributable to specific cost objects, then ABC should produce more accurate cost assignments than traditional cost systems. However, the cost of implementing and operating an ABC system (as described in Figure 3.1) is significantly more expensive than operating a direct cost or a traditional cost system. In particular, the training and software requirements may prohibit its adoption by small organisations. Also, ABC can mean considerable upheaval and concern, especially among middle managers, and this would need to be considered before implementation. There is also potential for confusion if two systems are operated.

Although traditional and non-absorption cost systems are less costly to operate, they have hidden costs. The partial costs reported by direct or variable cost systems and the distorted costs reported by traditional systems may also result in significant mistakes in decisions (such as dropping profitable products or continuing marketing unprofitable products) arising from the use of this information. If the cost of errors arising from using partial or distorted information generated from using these systems exceeds the additional costs of implementing and operating an ABC system, then there is a strong case for implementing ABC. In other words, ABC must meet the cost–benefit criterion.

Any evaluation of ABC should not be based purely on its product costing applications. To manage costs more effectively, ABC has been extended from product costing to a range of cost management applications. Organisations may choose to implement ABC for cost management rather than product costing, and any evaluation should take into account the benefits arising from all its applications rather than focusing only on product costing.

3.7 Limitations of ABC systems

This chapter has attempted to provide a conceptual understanding of ABC and explain why it produces more accurate reported costs than traditional cost systems. However, ABC does have some limitations. Where unit costs are calculated, ABC systems suffer from the same disadvantages as traditional cost systems by suggesting an inappropriate degree of variability. For example, to calculate unit product costs, batch level costs are divided by the number of units in the batch and product-sustaining costs are divided by the number of products produced. This unitising approach is an allocation which yields a constant average cost per unit of output which will differ depending on the selected output level. For decision-making, there is a danger that what started out as a non-volume-related activity cost will be translated into a cost which varies with production volume. Assuming a cost per set-up of £100 and a standard batch size of 100 units for a particular part, then the average set-up cost per part is £1. If a special order requiring the part for 50 units is received, then the batch size will differ from the standard batch size and the average cost of the set-up for processing the parts of £1 is not the appropriate cost to use for decision-making. If the special order requires one set-up, then the activity resources consumed will be £100 for an additional set-up.

To overcome such problems, Cooper (1997) advocates reporting total product costs rather than unit costs and distinguishing between unit, batch and product-sustaining costs. For example, if the price for a special order was being negotiated for 50 or 150 units which could be produced in a single batch, the relevant costs for the potential orders are the set-up cost of £100 for both order sizes plus the unit cost for the unit-level expenses multiplied by the order size. If the product for the order is already being made, no additional product-sustaining activities will be required and therefore the cost of these activities should not be taken into account in determining the relevant cost of the order. Therefore, Cooper argues that ABC systems provide a superior way of determining relevant cost, but care must be taken to avoid the pitfalls of ABC.

It was apparent from our discussion of cost hierarchies that many costs should not be assigned to individual products. The notion of cost hierarchies can also be applied with direct or traditional reporting systems. It is not unique to ABC. Bromwich and Bhimani (1994) suggest that such approaches have been widely used in Germany, where joint costs are assigned to that element of the product or organisational hierarchies at which they become avoidable with that segment of the organisation's activity. Both ABC and traditional systems use the same approach to assign unit-level costs to cost objects, and traditional systems can also use cost hierarchies for incorporating facility and other sustaining costs described in section 3.2. However, ABC uses more sophisticated methods for assigning batch-related and facility-sustaining costs to cost objects. If such costs are a small proportion of total costs, it is possible that traditional systems might assign similar costs to cost objects but with a system that is less expensive to operate.

A further problem is that the concept of managing unused capacity is fine for human resources, but it does not have the same impact for physical resources, such as the acquisition of plant and equipment. Human resources are more flexible and can be adjusted in small increments. Therefore the supply of resources can more easily be adjusted to the usage of resources. In contrast, physical resources are acquired or removed in lumpy amounts and large increments. If resources are supplied to cover a wide range of activity usage, there would have to be a dramatic change in activity for the supply to be changed. Therefore changes in resource usage would tend not be matched by a change in supply of resources and spending would remain unchanged. If the changes in physical resource usage arising from potential decisions does not have future cash-flow consequences, then any future cash-flow impact is likely to be dependent on the passage of time rather than usage. Thus there is unlikely to be a link between resource usage and spending, and the future cash-flow impact for most decisions will be zero. In other words, the cost of resource usage would be treated as fixed and unavoidable for most decisions, which is identical to how these costs would be treated adopting conventional wisdom.

The views expressed above depend on the extent to which changes in resource usage is likely to be matched by changes in the supply of resources for physical resources. This is likely to depend on the willingness of the top management team to vary the dimensions of the cost base, particularly with reference to the larger chunks in fixed capacity such as may relate to buildings, machines, mainframes, etc. If management believe that they can modify the shape of the cost base within the period under consideration, it is appropriate to view capacity as being variable and the cost of unused capacity can be used as a basis for reducing the cost base. In other words, it is legitimate to assume that there will be a link between resource usage and the supply of resources. If these conditions do not apply, it is appropriate to consider the cost of resource usage as being fixed and unavoidable.

4

Previous Research Related to the Study

4.1 Factors influencing the emergence of product costing research

Prior to the late 1980s researchers showed little interest in product costing. In recent years, surveys of product costing practices have been undertaken in the UK (Drury et al., 1993; Innes and Mitchell, 1995), the USA (Emore and Ness, 1991; Green and Amenkhienan, 1992), Finland (Lukka and Granlund, 1996), Sweden (Ask and Ax, 1992), Norway (Bjornenak, 1997a, 1997b), Japan (Yoshikawa et al., 1989) and Australia (Joye and Blayney, 1990, 1991).

The emergence of product costing research can be attributed to two factors. First, the changes in information technology, cost structures and the manufacturing and competitive environment resulted in increasing attention being given to product costing by both academics and practitioners. Second, the enormous amount of publicity given to criticisms of traditional product cost systems (most notably from the writings of Kaplan and Cooper) and the emergence of innovative ABC systems provided a further impetus for product costing research. This research has tended to focus on deriving empirical data relating to the usage of different costing methods (typically variable or absorption costing), the accuracy of product costs, the influence of financial accounting requirements on cost determination for decision-making and various issues relating to ABC. In particular, ABC research has tended to focus on the extent of usage, business applications, implementation problems and the identification of factors influencing success and failure of ABC.

4.2 Usage of different costing methods

With the exception of Finland and Norway, research relating to the usage of different costing methods tends to show that absorption costing dominates. The Drury et al. (1993) study reported that only 9 per cent of the respondents 'never' or 'rarely' used full costs. However, decisions were not based solely on full costs. Cost information was used in a flexible manner with both variable and full costs being used. Coates and Longden (1989) reported that most of the high-tech companies they studied in the USA and UK applied full costing. Further evidence indicating the use of full costing in the USA is reported by Hendricks (1988), with 85 per cent of the companies he studied using full costing. The results of Ask and Ax (1992) indicate that full costing dominates in Sweden, with 60 per cent of the firms applying it separately and 30 per cent using it simultaneously with variable costing. In contrast, the Finnish and Norwegian studies indicate that variable costing dominates. For example, Lukka and

Granlund (1996) report that 42 per cent of the companies used variable costing, 31 per cent used full (i.e. absorption) costing and 27 per cent used variable and absorption costing simultaneously.[1]

4.3 Accuracy of product costs

The evidence from the surveys suggests that simplistic product cost systems are widely used. These may not be sufficiently accurate when cost information is used either directly for decision-making or for attention-directing. Significant usage of single plant-wide overhead rates has been reported in some of the studies. For example, the percentage usages vary from 20 to 30 per cent in the UK (Drury and Tayles, 1994), US (Emore and Ness, 1991), Australian (Joye and Blayney, 1990, 1991) and Indian (Joshi,1998) surveys. In contrast, in Scandinavia only 5 per cent of the Finnish companies (Lukka and Granlund, 1996), one Norwegian company (Bjornenak, 1997b) and none of the Swedish companies sampled (Ask et al., 1996) used a single plant-wide rate. Zero usage of plant-wide rates was also reported from a survey of Greek companies (Ballas and Venieris, 1996).

With regard to the second stage of the two-stage allocation process, the surveys have reported that the vast majority of companies use a small number of volume-related allocation bases, typically direct labour and machine hours, with direct labour hours being the predominant method, even though most of the studies report that direct labour tends to be in the range of 10–15 per cent of total manufacturing costs.

4.4 Influence of financial accounting

A considerable amount of publicity has been given to the claim by Johnson and Kaplan (1987) that financial accounting dominates management accounting. In the USA, Cooper and Kaplan (1988) found that only one accounting system was used by the firms they visited. These accounting systems were used for cost and management accounting purposes, but they were designed primarily to meet financial accounting requirements. Johnson and Kaplan's claim is difficult to test empirically. However, evidence that manufacturing organisations use separate databases for financial accounting and management accounting would provide strong grounds for rejecting their claim.

Previous research suggests that most companies use a single database for meeting financial and management accounting requirements. The Drury et al. (1993) UK survey and the Emore and Ness (1991) US survey reported that most companies used the same product cost information for decision-making purposes that they used for financial statement inventory valuation. Lukka and Granlund (1996) reported that Finnish companies tended to use a single accounting system because of its simplicity and the avoidance of having to spend time reconciling figures between the financial and management accounting systems. Ask and Ax (1992) reported similar findings in

1 The terms full costing and absorption costing are used synonymously throughout this report

Sweden. Further support for organisations' preferences to use a single system is provided by Friedman and Lyne (1995), who found that some firms decided not to implement ABC because of the difficulty of making the ABC system their only system and the desire not to have two cost systems.

Even though the evidence suggests that most firms use a single accounting system, this does not support the claim that management accounting is subservient to financial accounting. The use of sophisticated cost accumulation systems (see section 5.2), that are over and above the level that are likely to be required for inventory valuation, would suggest that accounting systems are not designed primarily for meeting financial accounting requirements. Both financial and management accounting can exist within a single database and data can be selected, analysed, aggregated and reported in different ways to meet different needs (Burns et al., 1996). Costs which have been arbitrarily apportioned for stock valuation, and which are not relevant at the individual product level for decision-making (e.g. facility-sustaining costs), can be excluded when cost information is extracted for decision-making. Evidence, however, that manufacturing organisations use unsophisticated cost systems, or systems that do not enable cost information to be extracted in a flexible manner for decision-making, would indicate that the claim that financial accounting dominates management accounting cannot be rejected.

4.5 ABC usage

Significant variations in the usage of ABC both within the same country and across different countries have been reported. These differences may arise from the difficulty in precisely defining the difference between conventional cost systems and ABC systems and the specific period when the surveys were actually undertaken. For example, Dugdale and Jones (1997) identify a weak and a strong definition of ABC to partially explain the differences between their interpretation and Innes and Mitchell's (1995) interpretation of observations of the same firms relating to whether or not ABC was used for stock valuation. Survey evidence suggests that over the last decade there has been an increasing interest in ABC, but the rate of implementation has been slow. In the UK, surveys in the early 1990s reported adoption rates around 10 per cent (Innes and Mitchell, 1991; Nicholls, 1992; Drury et al., 1993). Similar adoption rates of 10 per cent were found in Ireland (Clarke, 1992) and 14 per cent in Canada (Armitage and Nicholson, 1993). In the USA, Green and Amenkhienan (1992) claimed that 45 per cent of firms used ABC to some extent. More recent surveys suggest higher ABC adoption rates. In the UK, reported usage was 20 per cent (Innes and Mitchell, 1995) and 21 per cent (Evans and Ashworth, 1996). In the USA, Hrisak (1996) reported that 53 per cent of survey respondents were using ABC and Shim and Sudit (1995) reported a usage rate of 27 per cent.

Other studies have examined the applications of ABC. Innes and Mitchell (1995) found that cost reduction was the most widely used application. Other widely used applications included product/service pricing, cost modelling and performance measurement/improvement. ABC was used for stock valuation by 29 per cent of ABC adopters, thus suggesting that the majority of ABC users have separate systems for stock valuation and management accounting applications.[2] According to Bjornenak (1997a) there has been little research on who adopts ABC and for what reasons. His survey indicated that 40 per cent of the responding companies had adopted ABC as an idea (i.e. they had implemented ABC or planned to do so). Different variables relating to cost structure, competition, existing cost systems, size and product diversity were tested as explanatory factors for the adoption of ABC, but only cost structure and size were found to be statistically significant.

2 Dugdale and Jones (1997) reviewed the same firms as Innes and Mitchell (1995) and claim that the application rate of 29 per cent was overstated.

5

Factors Influencing the Design of Cost Systems

5.1 Classification of cost systems

In order to gather information on the different types of cost accumulation systems that firms operate, cost systems were classified into the following four categories:

1 Systems that assign only direct variable costs (i.e. variable cost systems).
2 Systems that assign only direct variable costs and direct non-variable costs (i.e. direct cost systems).
3 Absorption cost systems that assign only direct costs plus a share of those indirect costs where cost drivers/allocation bases can be identified that are the causes of the costs varying in the long term.
4 Absorption cost systems that assign all costs identified within 3 above plus a share of those costs that are assigned using methods that do not rely on cause-and-effect allocations.

5.1.1 Variable cost systems

If variable cost systems are adopted, product profitability analysis will only report 'contributions to *all* fixed costs.' There is a danger that fixed costs will be ignored and low contribution margin products whose avoidable fixed costs exceed the reported contribution will continue to be marketed. However, if the reporting of low contribution margins is used as an attention-director to signal the need for undertaking special studies that incorporate avoidable fixed costs, then direct variable cost systems may be appropriate for product profitability analysis. If the costs reported by this cost system are used directly for decision-making, avoidable fixed costs will be ignored and there is a danger that wrong decisions will be made.

5.1.2 Direct cost systems

With direct cost systems, all direct costs that are uniquely attributable to specific products are included in the product costs. The costs of those joint resources that fluctuate in the long term according to the demand for them are not assigned to products and are thus excluded from the product profitability analysis. Product decisions are therefore assumed to be independent if product profitability analysis information is used directly for decision-making. Alternatively, the contribution to indirect fixed costs reported by the product profitability analysis can be used as an attention-directing device for identifying those low contribution products that require a more detailed analysis. At this stage an estimate can be made of the potential savings arising from the reduced consumption of 'joint resources' if the product, or combination of products, being investigated were discontinued.

5.1.3 Absorption cost systems using only cause-and-effect cost drivers

Where the third cost system is adopted, the cost system assigns indirect costs to cost objects using cost drivers that are the causes of resource consumption. The aim of cost systems within this category is not to assign any costs to specific cost objects if they require arbitrary allocations that are not based on cause-and-effect relationships. It is claimed that only ABC systems can meet this requirement. However, we do not exclude traditional cost systems, since the objective of cost systems included within this category is to assign only a share of those costs that fluctuate in the long term according to the demand for them using cause-and-effect cost drivers. Traditional cost systems may attempt to meet this requirement, albeit in an imperfect manner.

5.1.4 Absorption cost systems that assign costs using non-cause-and-effect allocation bases

In addition to assigning direct costs and those costs for which it is possible to establish cause-and-effect cost drivers, the cost system within the fourth category also assigns a share of those costs that are unavoidable and irrelevant to most decisions. Examples of such costs are facility-sustaining or infrastructure expenses which are necessary to stay in business. They provide general production and sales facilities and include items such as property and general administrative costs. Facility-sustaining costs are common and joint to *all* products marketed by the organisation and are likely to remain unchanged unless there is a dramatic expansion/contraction in the scale or scope of activities. Therefore, the assignment of such costs is likely to be inappropriate for product introduction or abandonment decisions. However, some of the facility-sustaining costs (e.g. plant depreciation) must be assigned to products in order to meet external financial accounting stock valuation requirements. Because it is not possible to establish cause-and-effect relationships for these costs, assignments must rely on more arbitrary allocation methods.

5.2 Different levels of sophistication and accuracy

5.2.1 Direct, variable and traditional cost systems

The four categories of cost systems described in the previous section can be further categorised by their level of sophistication. Direct and variable costing are partial cost systems. They accurately assign all direct costs to cost objects, but are unsophisticated in the sense that direct costing ignores indirect costs and variable costing ignores fixed costs. The cost systems within the third and fourth categories vary in their level of sophistication in assigning indirect costs to cost objects. Generally the sophistication (and also the accuracy) of a cost system in assigning indirect costs to cost objects is positively related to the number of cost pools and second-stage cost drivers that are used.

Traditional cost systems can vary from a single to many cost pools, but their distinguishing feature is that they rely on a small number of second-stage volume-based drivers such as direct labour hours, machine hours, materials cost and units of output. The most simplistic traditional system uses a single cost pool and cost driver to allocate indirect costs to cost objects. The resulting cost driver rate is frequently described as a plant-wide or a blanket overhead rate.

A single cost pool and cost driver can only be justified, in terms of reporting accurate product costs, when all products or services consume activity resources in similar proportions. Where the consumption of the different organisational activities by products or services varies significantly, separate cost centres/pools, each with its own cost driver rate, should be established in order to measure accurately resources consumed by cost objects. If only a small number of cost centres are established, it is likely that activities within a cost centre will not be homogeneous and, if the consumption of the activities by products/services within the cost centres varies, activity resource consumption will not be accurately measured. Therefore, in most situations, increasing the number of cost pools increases the accuracy of measuring the indirect costs consumed by cost objects. Organisations may, however, deliberately opt for a simplistic cost system that is easily understandable and which consumes few resources, but ideally the choice should be made on the basis of cost versus benefits criteria as described in section 3.6.

5.2.2 ABC systems

ABC systems also vary in terms of their sophistication and accuracy, and the number of cost pools and second-stage drivers that are established depends on a trade-off between the accuracy of the reported costs and the cost of measurement. To reduce the cost of measurement activities can be aggregated, but this will lead to the reporting of less accurate costs. For example, rather than classifying purchasing of materials as an activity, each of its constituent tasks could be classified as separate activities. However, this level of decomposition would involve the collection of a vast amount of data which is likely to be too costly. Alternatively, the purchasing activity might be merged with the material receiving, storing, issuing, moving and supplier payment activities to form a single material procurement and handling activity. This is likely to represent too high a level of aggregation because a single cost driver is unlikely to provide a satisfactory determinant of the cost of the activity.

The final choice of activities must be a matter of judgement, but it is likely to be influenced by factors such as the total cost of the activity centre and the ability of a single driver to provide a satisfactory determinant of the cost of the activity. Where the latter is not possible, further decomposition of the activity will be necessary. Kaplan and Cooper (1998, p. 99) suggest that relatively simple ABC systems have 30–50 activity cost pools and many different activity cost drivers.

5.2.3 Impact of transaction and duration cost drivers

The accuracy of the costs reported and the sophistication of a cost system cannot be entirely captured by the number of cost pools and drivers that are used. They are also influenced by the type of activity drivers that are used. Activity drivers normally consist of two types: transaction and duration. Transaction drivers, such as the number of purchase orders processed, number of customer orders processed, number of inspections performed and number of set-ups undertaken, all count the number of times an activity is performed. Transaction drivers are the least expensive type of cost driver, but they are also likely to be the least accurate because they assume that the same quantity of resources is required every time an activity is performed. However, if the variation in the amount of resources required by individual cost objects is not great, transaction drivers will provide a reasonably accurate measurement of activity resources consumed. If this condition does not apply, then duration cost drivers should be used.

Duration drivers represent the amount of time required to perform an activity. Examples of duration drivers include set-up hours and inspection hours. For example, if one product requires a short set-up time and another requires a long time, then using set-up hours as the cost driver will more accurately measure activity resource consumption than the transaction driver (number of set-ups) which assumes that an equal amount of activity resources are consumed by both products.

5.2.4 Distinguishing between ABC and non-ABC systems

It is apparent from previous research that difficulties can apply in distinguishing between ABC and non-ABC systems, and some researchers have questioned whether systems described by survey respondents as ABC are really ABC systems. For example, Dugdale and Jones (1997) identified a weak and strong definition of ABC to partially explain differences between their interpretation and the respondents' classification of the cost systems in their organisations. When asked to indicate whether their organisation had implemented an ABC system, some of the respondents to this study replied that partial ABC systems had been implemented. A classification difficulty arises because it is not easy to determine precisely at what point a traditional system becomes an ABC system. For example, should a system with a small number of highly aggregated activity pools relying on two second-stage volume drivers (direct labour and machine hours) and one non-volume-based driver be categorised as a traditional or an ABC system?

To overcome the above classification difficulties, and the fact that ABC systems are claimed to represent sophisticated and accurate reporting systems whereas traditional systems are depicted as being unsophisticated and reporting inaccurate costs, we have rejected classifying cost systems by these two categories. Instead, we have chosen to measure the sophistication and accuracy of cost systems in assigning costs to cost objects by using a combination of the number of cost pools and number of cost drivers that are used. This classification system is explained in section 9.2.

5.3 Factors influencing choice of cost systems

Apart from the ABC literature (e.g. Cooper, 1988b), which has provided guidelines on the conditions which are conducive for the adoption of ABC, no study has attempted to identify the factors that are likely to influence the choice of one of the four cost systems described at the start of this chapter or the level of sophistication that cost system designers should adopt to assign indirect costs to cost objects. We have identified the following potential explanatory variables that, in theory, ought to influence the design of cost systems:

1 Purposes for which the cost information is required.
2 Cost structure.
3 Competitive environment.
4 Product diversity.
5 Competitive strategy.
6 Size of organisation.
7 Type of organisation.

Questions were included within the questionnaire that sought to gather information on each of the above variables. The relationship between the potential explanatory factors, and the type and sophistication of the cost system, are shown in Figure 5.1. It can be seen that the potential explanatory variables can influence either, or both, the type or the sophistication of the cost system.

Figure 5.1 A model of cost systems design

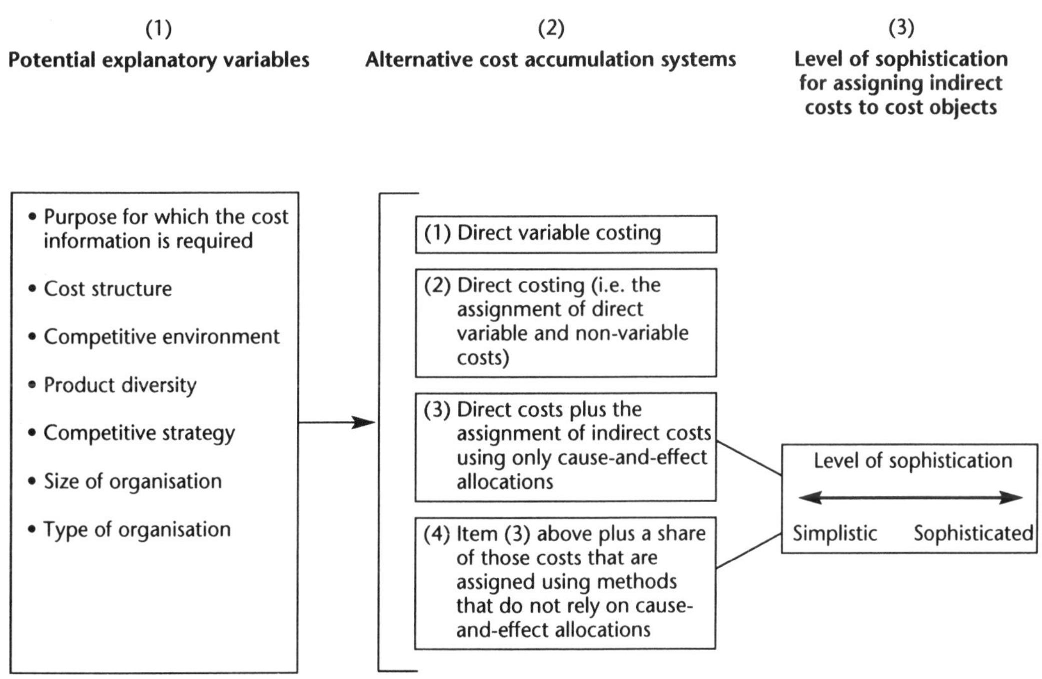

5.3.1 Purposes for which cost information is required

Organisations can choose to maintain a separate database for each of the major purposes for which cost information is required. Alternatively, they can maintain a single database and extract different information for different purposes.

Maintaining different databases for different purposes

If an organisation maintains different databases for different purposes, then the content of the databases will be influenced by the purpose for which the information is required. The research focuses on three purposes – stock valuation, profitability analysis and pricing decisions – to ascertain whether a separate cost accumulation system is used for each of these purposes. For those organisations that are faced with meeting stock valuation requirements, external financial regulations require companies to adopt the fourth cost accumulation system described at the start of this chapter and shown in Figure 5.1. Since the objective is to allocate costs between cost of goods sold and inventories at the *aggregate* level, accurate *individual* product costs may not be required and an unsophisticated cost system may suffice.

Periodic profitability analysis can be used either directly, or as an attention-directing mechanism, for signalling the need to undertake special studies for making key strategic decisions relating to outsourcing, redesigning or discontinuing products or services. Decisions arising from product profitability analysis are unlikely to alter facility-sustaining costs and the fourth cost accumulation system is therefore likely to be inappropriate for profitability analysis. If the third cost accumulation system shown in Figure 5.1 is adopted, the system must be sufficiently sophisticated to ensure that distorted product costs are not reported that lead to incorrect decisions. Alternatively, organisations may choose to assign only direct or variable costs to cost objects for routine periodic profitability analysis.

For product pricing decisions where no competitive market price exists and cost-plus pricing is used as a mechanism to determine selling prices, organisations may seek to ensure that all costs are covered and assign most of their costs (including facility-sustaining costs) to products. In other words, the fourth cost accumulation shown in Figure 5.1 should be used. Theory would also suggest that sophisticated systems ought to be used, since undercosting will lead to the acceptance of unprofitable business and overcosting may lead to the loss of profitable business. Furthermore, the allocation method used directly influences the proportion of the cost of the joint resources borne by different customers. Thus arbitrary allocation methods should be avoided and an attempt made to accurately measure the resources consumed by different customers based on the benefits received from the usage of common facilities.

Maintaining a single database

Instead of establishing separate cost accumulation systems for different purposes, appropriate cost information can be extracted from a single database. When stock valuation or cost-plus pricing are significant issues, the database should consist of the fourth cost accumulation system shown in Figure 5.1. For stock valuation, all manufacturing costs, including facility-sustaining costs where cause-and-effect relationships cannot be established, must be assigned to products. For product pricing decisions we have suggested in the above paragraph that there is a strong argument for allocating a share of all costs to products or services. Such allocations will also involve the allocation of some costs where cause-and-effect allocation bases cannot be established. For profitability analysis, however, it may appropriate to extract only direct costs and those indirect costs that are assigned using cause-and-effect allocations. Alternatively, if it is considered that indirect cost assignments are not sufficiently accurate, they can be stripped out and only direct costs incorporated within the profitability analysis. Where stock valuation and cost-plus pricing are not important, profitability analysis requirements should determine the content and accuracy of the database. Thus, where a single database is maintained, the purpose for which the information is required will influence what is extracted from the database. Also, different levels of accuracy for different purposes cannot be maintained within a single database.

5.3.2 Cost structures

Where the proportion of indirect costs within an organisation's cost structure is high, direct cost systems will trace only a small proportion of costs to cost objects and such systems are likely to be inappropriate for profitability analysis or pricing. Kaplan and Cooper (1998, p. 101) advocate that organisations with high indirect costs should assign these costs using sophisticated systems, since unsophisticated systems are likely to report distorted costs. In these circumstances they argue that ABC systems should be implemented. Conversely, where the proportion of indirect costs is low, direct costing may be appropriate or, if indirect costs are assigned to cost objects, unsophisticated traditional cost systems using a small number of cost pools and cost drivers may not result in the reporting of seriously distorted costs. We therefore hypothesise that there is a positive relationship between the level of indirect costs and the use of sophisticated cost systems that assign indirect costs to cost objects.

5.3.3 Competitive environment

Several studies have examined the relationship between the design and use of management accounting systems and the intensity of competition (Simons, 1990; Libby and Waterhouse, 1996). The results of these studies suggest that companies facing intensely competitive market environments tend to employ relatively sophisticated management accounting systems. Cooper (1988b) has also identified that organisations facing fierce competition should implement ABC. It is argued that firms operating in a more competitive environment have a greater need for sophisticated cost systems that more accurately assign costs to products, services and customers because competitors are more likely to take advantage of any errors from managers having to rely on inaccurate cost information to make decisions. We therefore hypothesise that the intensity of competition is positively related to the adoption of more sophisticated cost systems.

5.3.4 Product diversity

Cooper (1988a) has argued that product and volume diversity are major factors that result in the reporting of distorted product costs by traditional cost systems. Product diversity applies when products consume activity resources in different proportions. Greater product diversity requires more sophisticated cost systems to capture the variation in resource consumption by different products. Simplistic cost systems that rely on a small number of cost pools and drivers are unlikely to capture the diversity of consumption of activity resources by cost objects. Significantly distorted product costs are therefore likely to be reported when high diversity exists.

Besides product diversity, products may also be subject to volume diversity. Volume diversity occurs when products are manufactured in different batch sizes. To capture volume diversity, a sophisticated cost system is required that establishes separate cost pools for batch-level activities and incorporates non-volume-based cost drivers that measure the consumption of resources by batch sizes rather than volume. If volume-related cost drivers are used, most of the costs will be assigned to high-volume products which are likely to be produced in a smaller number of high-volume batches. Conversely, low-volume products whose output may be derived from a large number of low-volume batches will be assigned a smaller share of batch-level activities. Where volume diversity is high, low-volume products are likely to be undercosted and high-volume products overcosted.

The variations in consumption of activity resources can be extended to other cost objects besides products. For example, high customer diversity exists in an organisation which services customers who order high-volume, standard products which require few special demands and other customers who order low-volume, non-standard products requiring large quantities of before- and after-sales support.

It is very difficult to measure the diversity of resource consumption by cost objects. The survey questionnaire included questions relating directly to the variations in support department resource consumption by cost objects and variations in sales volumes. Other measures of diversity were also included within the questionnaire, such as degree of customised and standardised products and services, number of items within the cost object that are costed, and the percentage of items within the cost objects that are discontinued or introduced. This information was collected in order to test the hypothesis that higher diversity in resource consumption is positively related to the adoption of more sophisticated cost systems.

We also hypothesise that the number of items costed will influence the type of cost accumulation system that is adopted. Where only a small number of items are costed, the number of potential decisions is manageable by undertaking special studies. Only a few combinations of products or customers will need to be examined. Therefore there is less need for the cost system to routinely assign a share of those resources that fluctuate according to the demand for them to cost objects. Decisions are likely to relate to a single product, service or customer (or a small combination of these) and all potential combinations can be captured within special studies to identify avoidable fixed costs. We conclude that where an organisation costs a small number of items, interdependencies within the items costed are less likely to exist and there is a greater likelihood that direct cost systems will be adopted for profitability analysis.

5.3.5 Competitive strategy

Competitive strategy describes how a business chooses to compete in its industry and tries to achieve a competitive advantage relative to its competitors. Porter (1985) suggests that a firm has a choice of three generic strategies in order to achieve sustainable competitive advantage. They are:

- *cost leadership,* whereby an enterprise aims to be the lowest-cost producer within the industry;
- *differentiation,* whereby the enterprise seeks to offer some unique dimension in its products/service that is valued by customers and which can command a premium price;
- *focus,* which involves seeking advantage in a narrow segment of the market, either by way of cost leadership or by product differentiation.

Most of the research that has addressed Porter's strategy variables has focused on the use of accounting information for control and performance measurement rather than product cost systems. In particular, the research has examined the control aspects between businesses pursuing cost leadership and differentiation strategies.

Companies pursuing a cost leadership strategy offer a limited range of high-volume products at the lowest possible price, whereas companies pursuing a differentiation strategy offer customised products or products with unique functionality. For a differentiation strategy to be successful, the price premiums from offering customised products and services must exceed the added cost of being unique. For example, Porter (1985) states:

> Differentiation leads to superior performance if the price premium achieved exceeds any added costs of being unique.... A differentiator must always seek ways of differentiating that lead to a price premium greater than the cost of differentiating. A differentiator cannot ignore its cost position, because its premium prices will be nullified by a markedly inferior cost position (p. 120, p. 14).

Companies that follow a differentiated strategy and use direct or variable cost systems, or unsophisticated absorption cost systems, will not be able to estimate the incremental costs of achieving differentiation. They need a sophisticated cost system that accurately measures the costs of product and volume diversity that stem from following a differentiation strategy. Without such a system they run the risk of not being able to determine whether the higher revenues generated from their products or services exceeds the extra costs associated with differentiation. Therefore we hypothesise that organisations following a differentiation strategy will have more sophisticated cost systems.

5.3.6 Size of organisational unit

Previous studies have noted a positive relationship between company size and management accounting system sophistication. In particular, studies of ABC adoption rates have shown that adoption is much higher in larger organisations (Innes and Mitchell, 1995; Bjornenak, 1997a). A possible reason for this is that larger organisations have relatively greater access to resources to experiment with the introduction of more sophisticated systems. Several surveys have also indicated that an important factor limiting the implementation of more sophisticated management accounting systems is the prohibitive cost (Innes and Mitchell, 1995; Shields, 1995). As larger organisations have more resources to develop innovative systems, it is also more likely that they will be able to implement more sophisticated cost systems. Larger organisations are also more likely to have a larger and more diversified range of activities leading to greater product, service and customer diversity, thus creating the need for more sophisticated cost systems to measure resource consumption by different cost objects. We therefore conclude that organisational size is positively related to the adoption of more sophisticated cost systems.

5.3.7 Type of organisation

Kaplan and Cooper (1998, p. 231) suggest that service companies are ideal candidates for ABC, even more than manufacturing companies. Their justification for this statement is that most costs in service organisations are fixed and indirect. In contrast, manufacturing companies can trace important components (direct materials and direct labour) of costs to individual products. Service organisations must also supply most of their resources in advance and fluctuations in the usage of activity resources by individual services and customers do not influence short-term spending to supply the resources. Such costs are treated by simplistic cost systems as fixed and irrelevant for most decisions. This resulted in a situation where profitability analysis was not considered helpful for decision-making. Furthermore, until recently many service organisations were either government-owned monopolies or operated in a highly regulated, protected and non-competitive environment. These organisations were not subject to any great pressures to improve profitability by identifying and eliminating non-profit-making activities. Cost increases could also be absorbed by increasing the prices of services to customers. Little attention was therefore given to developing cost systems that accurately measured the costs and profitability of individual services.

Privatisation of government-owned monopolies, deregulation, intensive competition and an expanding product range created the need for service organisations to develop management accounting systems that enabled them to understand their cost base and determine the sources of profitability for their products/services, customers and markets. Many service organisations have therefore only recently implemented management accounting systems. They have had the advantage of not having to meet some of the constraints imposed on manufacturing organisations, such as having to meet financial accounting stock valuation requirements or the reluctance to scrap or change existing cost systems that might have become embedded in organisations. Furthermore, service organisations have been implementing new systems at the same time as the deficiencies of traditional systems were being widely publicised and new insights were beginning to emerge on how cost systems could be viewed as resource consumption models which could be used to make decisions on adjusting the spending on the supply of resources to match resource consumption.

All the above factors lead us to conclude that compared with manufacturing organisations service organisations are more likely to adopt sophisticated management accounting systems.

6

An Overview of the Study

6.1 Missing information on cost systems

Previous studies have tended not to distinguish between the different purposes (e.g. stock valuation, profitability analysis, pricing, and product mix decisions) for which cost information is required. Where a single database is maintained there is a danger that respondents will specify the details that are maintained in the database rather than the information that is extracted for a specific purpose. If the purpose for which the information is required is not made explicit by the researcher, there is a danger that misleading results will be reported.

Most of the previous surveys on product costing have tended to describe product costing practices rather than explain them. Little is known about the impact of potential explanatory variables on observed practices. Also, previous studies have focused mainly on manufacturing organisations, whereas the issues extend to all types of organisations and business categories (e.g. manufacturing, retail, service, financial and commercial). Where non-manufacturing organisations have been studied they have tended to be studied separately. There is a need to study manufacturing and non-manufacturing organisation within a single survey, so that replies to common questions at a single point in time can be compared.

It is also apparent from previous studies that profitability analysis is widely used in organisations. A survey of Australian companies by Chenhall and Langfield-Smith (1998) reported that product profitability analysis was one of the areas where the companies would place relatively greater future emphasis. Cooper (1997) has stressed that one of the major roles of ABC is as a resource usage model to develop profitability maps (i.e. periodic profitability analysis by cost objects) for focusing management attention. Despite the increasing interest in profitability analysis, little is known about the nature, role and content of profitability analysis in organisations.

In order to explore the above and other issues a postal questionnaire survey was undertaken to provide information on the following:

1. The extent to which different explanatory variables influence the design of cost systems currently used by UK organisations. In particular, the impact of the explanatory variables on the costing method and the level of sophistication is explored.
2. The nature, content and role of product profitability analysis in managing an organisation's existing product mix. For example:
   (a) the extent to which organisations periodically analyse profits by products/ services, customers, locations, etc.;

(b) the level of importance attached to profitability analysis in signalling the need to make key strategic decisions relating to outsourcing, redesigning or discontinuing the activities outlined in (a);

(c) the extent to which other mechanisms are used to signal the need to make the key strategic decisions identified in (b) above;

(d) the extent to which a hierarchical approach of profitability assessment is used and, if so, the critical profitability measures in the hierarchy that organisations use for decision-making;

(e) whether product profitability analysis is used directly for decision-making or for attention-directing for signalling the need for a more detailed financial analysis (i.e. special studies);

(f) the content of the information that is used in the special studies;

(g) whether information is reported at the product line level, or at the individual product level and, where profitability is analysed by the individual products within the product line, how joint product line costs are dealt with.

3 The treatment of facility-sustaining costs. If facility-sustaining costs are allocated to cost pools in the first stage of the two-stage allocation procedure, and not separately identified, there is a danger that they will be hidden within other costs when cost driver rates are established. Therefore the reported costs will suggest an inappropriate degree of variability and misleading information may be presented.

4 The extent to which companies use a single database for which different costs are extracted for meeting different requirements or the extent to which separate systems are used for generating information for different types of decisions.

5 The methods used to measure capacity levels to establish the denominator levels for calculating cost driver rates.

6 The extent to which organisations implement activity-based systems and do not extend it to product costing. There is evidence to suggest that the cost management applications may outweigh the product costing applications (Innes and Mitchell, 1995). Gosselin (1997) identifies three levels of activity management – activity analysis, activity cost analysis and ABC. Activity analysis and activity cost analysis can be accomplished without implementing an activity-based product cost system.

6.2 Sample selection

Because of the specialist nature of the survey it was necessary to ensure that those completing the questionnaire were qualified to do so. Therefore we addressed the questionnaire personally to accountants who had been qualified members of the Chartered Institute of Management Accountants (CIMA) for a period of more than five years. This information was derived from the membership database of CIMA. The respondents were selected on the basis of their job titles, the aim being to select those respondents who were likely to have specialist knowledge relating to the information requested within the questionnaire.

The selection of the organisations to be included in the sample focused on business units. Often samples are drawn from a sample of listed companies (e.g. from 'The Times 1000') and questionnaires are addressed to corporate headquarters of the group reporting entity. Many of the aspects that are of most interest to this survey centre on cost systems operated at the business unit level, rather than the corporate level. For these reasons we rejected selecting a sample of listed companies from a database similar to 'The Times 1000'.

Because our aim was to concentrate on companies with established cost systems we selected a sample consisting of all organisations whose objectives were profit-making and which employed two or more CIMA-qualified members with more than five years' post-qualification experience. Thus, charity, local authority and public sector organisations whose objectives were not profit-making were excluded from the analysis. This selection process resulted in a sample of 631 organisations.

Selecting a sample consisting only of business units that employ two or more CIMA-qualified accountants with more than five years' experience is likely to exclude organisations that do not have well-established management accounting systems. In particular, smaller organisations are likely to be excluded. Although members of professional bodies, other than CIMA, are employed as management accountants in UK companies, our analysis of the membership of CIMA and other accountancy bodies suggests that the vast majority of UK companies with established management accounting systems will employ at least two CIMA-qualified management accountants. We therefore believe that our sample constitutes a representative sample of organisations with established management accounting systems. The findings, however, cannot be generalised to apply to organisations that do not meet the criteria we have used to establish the sample.

6.3 Data collection

In December 1998 a postal survey was undertaken which aimed to gather empirical data on the costing practices of UK companies. Before mailing, eight company visits were undertaken to pilot test the questionnaire and discuss issues relating to the replies. The final version of the questionnaire contained 18 pages and included 72 questions. A copy of the questionnaire can be found in Appendix II.

Because the questionnaire was lengthy and the subject was of a specialist nature, we initially sent an introductory letter to all the potential respondents which explained the rationale and objectives of the research and asked them to indicate whether or not they would be prepared to participate in the survey. We also enclosed with the introductory letter a short one-page initial questionnaire (see Appendix I) and requested both those agreeing and not agreeing to participate in the survey to complete it. Our aim was to gather information on the participating and non-participating organisations to check for non-response bias. Since one of the major areas of the survey related to profitability analysis, the initial questionnaire contained a question on the extent to which profitability analysis was used. Other questions related to the size and business sector of the organisation, extent of cost-plus pricing and whether costs were accumulated for stock valuation.

Replies were received from 350 respondents (an initial response rate of 55 per cent), with 170 agreeing (49 per cent of the respondents) and 180 (51 per cent) not agreeing to participate. Most of the reasons given for non-participation specified lack of time, although less than 5 per cent of the respondents stated that they did not consider the research was relevant to their organisation and a small number of organisations ($N = 10$) had ceased to operate. Responses for participants and non-participants were compared using either the Mann–Whitney or chi-square non-parametric tests. There was no evidence of non-response bias. To increase the final response rate we telephoned a random sample of 100 non-respondents of which 90 agreed to participate in the research. The total number of respondents agreeing to complete the full questionnaire was therefore 260, but only 187 respondents returned the completed full questionnaire despite reminders to the 73 respondents who initially indicated that they were prepared to participate in the study. This represents a response rate of 30.1 per cent to the full sample of 631 organisations less 10 ceasing to exist. To clarify the responses and discuss issues arising from the questionnaire replies, 72 per cent of the 187 respondents were contacted by telephone.

The full questionnaire included most of the questions that were included in the one-page initial questionnaire. Further tests comparing the responses to these questions for the 187 respondents completing the full questionnaire with the 180 non-participating respondents completing the initial questionnaire did not provide any evidence of non-response bias. In addition, the early and late replies to the full questionnaire were compared. No evidence of non-response bias was found from this comparison.

Thus, out of our initial usable sample of 621 organisations, we do not have any data relating to 254 of the organisations that were included in the sample. The latter figure is derived from deducting the sum of 187 respondents completing the full and 180 completing the initial questionnaire, from the usable sample of 621 organisations. Ideally, we would have liked to compare the attributes of the responding organisations (size, business sector, etc.) with all the organisations in our sample that did not complete the full questionnaire, in order to provide a complete check for non-response bias. However, the tests described above that we have undertaken do provide strong evidence to suggest that non-response bias is unlikely to exist. Nevertheless, the imperfections that we have described should be taken into account when generalising the results to all the organisations within the sample.

6.4 Questionnaire content

In the letter accompanying the questionnaire the respondents were asked to answer only those questions that were relevant to their organisation and to omit any questions where they were unsure of the response for their organisation. Therefore the responses to individual questions may not be equivalent to the total number of completed questionnaires. Throughout the report the number of responses to individual questions is denoted *N*.

The questionnaire was divided into seven sections. The first section contained general questions relating to the organisations' cost systems and the product costing environment. Information on the potential explanatory variables was mostly collected within this section. The second section focused on profitability analysis and decision-making, the third on cost accumulation for stock valuation and the fourth on cost information for setting selling prices. The fifth section included questions relating to how activity levels were determined for establishing cost driver rates. Details about the organisational units (e.g. size, business sector, etc.) were collected in the sixth section. The final section collected information about the respondent. For the second, third and fourth sections the respondents were asked to relate their answers only to the purposes specified within the section (i.e. profitability analysis, stock valuation and setting selling prices). Respondents were also asked to confirm whether or not the costs accumulated, or used, for one purpose were the same as those used for other purposes.

7

Survey Findings Relating to Cost Information for Periodic Profitability Analysis

7.1 Respondents' organisational and professional background

Information on the respondents' organisational and professional background is presented in Table 7.1. This table shows that the respondents are employed in a number of different types of industry, in organisations of varying sizes and at different locations within the organisations. The majority of respondents (68 per cent) have been qualified accountants for more than ten years. The respondents were also asked if it would be possible for a meeting to be arranged to discuss some of the issues raised by the survey. Of the 182 responses to this question, 48 per cent stated that a meeting would be possible. The wide range of companies covered and the length of post-qualification experience suggest that the responses provide insights into cost system design in UK organisations. Also, the fact that approximately 50 per cent were prepared to provide time for a meeting to discuss the issues arising from the research suggests that the survey content is of interest to practitioners.

In section 6.2 it was pointed out that the sample selection aimed to include only organisations with established formal cost systems. By selecting a sample, based on organisations employing two or more CIMA members with more than five years' post-qualification experience, many smaller companies that are not likely to have well-established cost systems were omitted.[1] The sample also excluded organisations whose objectives were not profit-making, typically service organisations. These factors may account for the fact that only 31 per cent of the responding organisations were from the service sector, even though this sector accounts for approximately 60 per cent of UK gross domestic product.

---

1 The sample was selected from organisations employing two or more CIMA members with more than five years' post-qualification experience, but recipients were asked to pass the questionnaire to another suitable person within the organisation if they were not the most appropriate person to complete the questionnaire. This explains why 6 per cent of the respondents shown in Table 7.1 had less than five years' post-qualifying experience.

Table 7.1 Information on the respondents' organisational and professional background

	No. of cases[a]	Percentage
Organisational background		
Annual sales turnover		
£0–£25m	15	8
£26–£50m	24	13
£51–£75m	19	10
£76–£100m	19	10
£101m–£200m	27	15
£201m–£300m	14	8
Over £300m	68	36
	186	100
Proportion of group sales turnover		
0–10%	76	46
11–20%	24	14
21–30%	14	8
31–40%	11	7
41–50%	11	7
Over 50%	29	18
	165	100
Business type		
Manufacturing	128	69
Retail	9	5
Service	26	14
Financial and commercial	15	8
Other	7	4
	185	100
Location of head office		
UK	111	64
Overseas	62	36
	173	100
Group structure		
Organisation part of a group structure	173	93
Organisation not part of a group structure	13	7
	186	100
Stock Exchange listing		
Listed	111	64
Non-listed	62	36
	173	100
Personal Background		
Location in organisation		
Group head office	45	24
Divisional head office	63	34
Operating unit	74	40
No group or operating unit structure	5	2
	187	100
Post-qualification experience		
Less than 2 years[a]	3	2
2–5 years[b]	8	4
5–10 years	47	26
Over 10 years	124	68
	182	100

[a] 187 completed questionnaires were received, but for some responses relevant details were not provided by the respondents. Therefore the number of cases does not equal 187 for all of the replies.

[b] The sample was selected from organisations employing two or more CIMA members with more than five years' post-qualification experience, but recipients were asked to pass the questionnaire to another suitable person within the organisation if they were not the most appropriate person to complete the questionnaire. This explains why 6 per cent of the respondents shown in the above table had less than five years' post-qualifying experience.

7.2 Maintaining separate databases for different purposes

Pursuing the line of different costs for different purposes the respondents were asked to indicate whether a separate database was maintained for accumulating costs for periodic profitability analysis, stock valuation and setting selling prices. Of the 187 responding organisations, 136 (73 per cent) stated that costs were accumulated for stock valuation, and that the value was significant for financial reporting. Only 12 out of the 136 organisations (9 per cent) maintained a separate database for stock valuation and extracted cost information for decision-making from other databases within the organisation. The remaining 91 per cent stated that a single database was maintained from which appropriate cost information was extracted to provide the required information for both stock valuation and decision-making. Cost-plus pricing was used by 60 per cent of the responding organisations as a mechanism to determine selling prices for some of their products or services. All of the organisations that maintained a separate database for stock valuation did not use information extracted from this database for pricing decisions.

7.3 Cost structures

An analysis of total costs by direct and indirect costs for each type of organisation is shown in Table 7.2. Previous surveys of the cost structures of manufacturing companies in the UK (Drury et al., 1993), USA (Green and Amenkhienan, 1992), Australia (Joye and Blayney, 1990) and Belgium (Kerremans et al., 1991) have reported remarkably similar results in terms of cost structures. They all report that direct costs and indirect costs averaged approximately 75 per cent and 25 per cent respectively of total manufacturing costs.

Table 7.2 Analysis of cost structures by business types

Business Type	*% Average direct costs*	*% Average indirect costs*	*% Standard deviation*
Manufacturing (*N* = 122)[a]	70.63	29.37	14.42
Retail (*N* = 10)	73.20	27.80	14.50
Service (*N* = 26)	71.96	28.04	18.35
Financial and commercial (*N* = 12)	51.58	48.42	26.35
Other (*N* = 6)	80.17	19.83	8.98
All organisations (*N* = 176)	69.94	30.06	16.63

[a] For manufacturing organisations, direct costs were analysed as follows: direct materials (50.63 per cent), direct labour (13.31 per cent), non-manufacturing direct (6.67 per cent).

The results reported in Table 7.2 relate to direct and indirect costs as a percentage of all costs, rather than manufacturing costs, as reported in the studies cited in the above paragraph. It is apparent from this table that, apart from financial and commercial organisations, the cost structures are fairly similar for the remaining organisations. A comparison of the responses of the financial and commercial organisations with the remaining organisations for cost structures indicated that the responses were significantly different at the 5 per cent level.[2] Further analysis indicated a variation in the responses, with 11 per cent of the responding organisations (excluding financial and commercial) reporting indirect costs of 10 per cent or less of total costs. Alternatively, indirect costs exceeded 40 per cent for 19 per cent of these organisations. For financial and commercial organisations the corresponding percentages were 8 per cent and 58 per cent.

7.4 Role of profitability analysis

The questionnaire included questions relating to the role and content of profitability analysis for discontinuation, redesign, outsourcing and cost reduction decisions. Table 7.3 shows the frequency of routine profitability analysis by products/services, components, customers and locations. It can be seen that 91 per cent of the respondents analysed profits at least on an annual basis. It is clear from Table 7.3 that profitability analysis is widely used, with most of the respondents analysing profits by more than one category at frequent intervals. Five organisations indicated that they did not undertake any type of profitability analysis. Given that organisations analyse profits by more than one category, the respondents were asked to select at the start of the profitability analysis section of the questionnaire the category which they considered was the most important for their organisation and relate all their responses to the remaining questions on profitability analysis to their chosen category. The categories chosen were products/services (81 per cent), customers (5 per cent), locations (9 per cent) and other (5 per cent).

Table 7.3 Extent and frequency of profitability analysis ($N = 185$)

	Monthly	Quarterly	Six-monthly	Annually	> 1 yr	Not routinely analysed
	%	%	%	%	%	%
Products/services	75	9	4	3		9
Components	25	4	3	4		64
Customers/ customer categories	47	11	7	9	2	24
Locations	69	4		3		24
Other	7					93

2 The non-parametric Mann–Whitney two-tailed U-test rejected the null hypothesis that there is no difference in cost structures between financial and commercial organisations and the remaining organisations at the 5 per cent level.

Table 7.4 Number of different cost objects to which the cost system assigns costs (analysed by respondents' chosen profitability category)

	<6 %	*6–20* %	*21–80* %	*81–200* %	*201–500* %	*Over 500* %
Products/services (*N* = 148)	3	8	12	16	17	44
Customers (*N* = 9)			33	33		34
Locations (*N* = 17)	12	29	6	23	24	6
Other (*N* = 10)		30	10		20	40

Table 7.5 Ranking of importance of factors in signalling the need to make key decisions (*N* = 185)

	% Ranking most important	*% Ranking second most important*	*% Ranking third most important*	*% Respondents not ranking in top 3 categories*
Profitability analysis shows insufficient profit	46	19	18	17
Predicted sales volume trend	18	27	20	35
Selling price decline	16	21	18	45
Market share decline	6	15	17	62
Past sales volume decline	5	7	16	72
Introduction of superior product by competitor	8	9	11	72
Other	1	2		97

The number of different cost objects that costs are assigned to is shown in Table 7.4. This table indicates that most organisations assign costs to a large number of items within each cost object. We therefore conclude that it is not feasible, in most cases, to routinely undertake special studies for each individual item (e.g. products/services) within a cost object or combination of items within the cost object. An attention-directing mechanism is required that identifies those potentially unprofitable activities where more detailed special studies are required. Periodic routine profitability analysis meets this requirement.

The respondents were asked to indicate the role played by profitability analysis. Periodic profitability analysis was used directly for decision-making by 19 per cent of the respondents, and the remaining 81 per cent stated that it was used as an attention-directing mechanism for signalling the need for a more detailed analysis to be undertaken. It was apparent in the telephone conversations with some of those respondents who stated that periodic profitability analysis was used directly for decision-making *did* undertake further financial analysis. It is therefore likely that the responses relating to the use of periodic profitability analysis directly for decision-making are overstated.

Other mechanisms, besides profitability analysis, can also be used to signal the need to make key decisions. In order to ascertain the relative importance of profitability analysis the respondents were asked to rank, according to the order of importance, the top three of a list of factors that were used to signal the need to make key decisions relating to cost reduction, redesigning, outsourcing or discontinuing items within their chosen cost objective. The respondents also had the opportunity to insert additional factors besides those listed in the questionnaire. The responses are reported in Table 7.5. It is apparent from this table that profitability analysis is considered the most important factor, although it could be viewed as surprising that 17 per cent did not rank profitability analysis, given that the questionnaires were completed by accountants. However, it is also reassuring that accountants considered factors other than short-term profitability measures as important signals for the need to make key decisions.

A further question was asked to clarify the importance of profitability analysis. On a scale of 1 (not important) to 7 (vitally important), the respondents were asked to indicate the importance of profitability analysis in indicating the need to make key decisions for items within their chosen cost object. The average score was 5.30 (N = 184 and standard deviation = 1.84), with 55 per cent entering a score of 6 or 7.

7.5 Cost information used within profitability analysis

Having focused on the importance of profitability analysis, information was collected on the costs accumulated for routine periodic profitability analysis. Data was collected on the four cost categories described in Chapter 5. They were:

1. Direct variable costs that can be specifically traced to items within the cost objects (100 per cent).
2. Direct variable and non-variable costs (e.g. depreciation) that can be specifically traced to items within the cost objects (93 per cent).
3. Indirect costs assigned to cost objects where cost drivers can be identified that are the causes of the costs varying in the long term (86 per cent).
4. Indirect costs assigned to cost objects where cost drivers cannot be identified that are the causes of the costs varying in the long term. Costs are therefore assigned using methods that do not rely on cause-and-effect allocations (79 per cent).

Costs in the third category typically consist of batch and product-sustaining activities, whereas costs in the fourth category consist of facility-sustaining/infrastructure costs. The figures in parentheses refer to the percentage of respondents assigning costs within each category. All organisations assigned direct variable costs. Given that 86 per cent assigned some form of indirect costs, the above analysis implies that 14 per cent assign *only* direct costs to cost objectives. A further 7 per cent (i.e. the differences between rows 3 and 4 in the above paragraph) assign only those indirect costs where cost drivers can be ascertained that are the causes of costs varying in the long term. The remaining 79 per cent assigned direct costs and indirect costs using both cause-and-effect cost drivers and drivers where cause-and-effect relationships cannot be established. In the telephone interviews with some of the respondents whose organisations only assigned direct costs, it was indicated that this was only for routine periodic profitability reporting. Indirect costs were still assigned to cost objects for other purposes and sometimes used when detailed special studies were undertaken.

Costs in the third and fourth categories, described above, may be merged when they are allocated to cost objects and thus may not be separately identifiable. The respondents were therefore asked to indicate whether the costs in each of the above four categories were separately identified and reported within the cost system. In other words, one question focused on which costs were assigned to cost objects within the cost accumulation system and another asked whether the specific category of costs was separately reported within the cost system. Virtually all (94 per cent) of those 93 per cent of the respondents that indicated that direct variable and non-variable direct costs were assigned to cost objects separately reported these two categories of costs. Of the 79 per cent of responding organisations (i.e. $N = 147$) that assigned both cause-and-effect indirect costs and those indirect costs where cause-and-effect relationships cannot be established, 56 per cent ($N = 81$) could distinguish between the two categories of costs and the remaining 44 per cent ($N = 66$) combined them together as a lump sum allocation. Thus, 79 per cent of the respondents compiled some form of absorption cost and 56 per cent of these respondents had the potential to use the cost information in a flexible manner.

The above findings indicate that the cost systems routinely separately report short-term incremental cost. Furthermore, since the reporting systems for the majority of respondents also distinguished between the different categories of indirect costs, the potential exists for cost information to be used in a flexible manner. Thus, it is possible that criticisms by various commentators relating to the widespread naive use of full costs that incorporate arbitrary cost allocations may have been overstated because they may have based their criticisms on what is accumulated within the cost system rather than what is reported or extracted from the system for decision-making requirements.

7.6 Importance of alternative reported profitability measures

Because different categories of costs can be extracted from the database it is possible to report a hierarchy of profitability measures within the profitability analysis. The respondents were therefore asked to indicate (either directly for decision-making or as an attention-directing device) which items within a list of profitability measures were the most important or second most important measure for these purposes.[3] It can be seen from Table 7.6 that the highest percentage of respondents ranked sales less direct or variable costs (contribution) as the most important measure. Rows 3 and 4 in Table 7.6 include arbitrary allocations. Row 3 provided the opportunity for respondents to signify a profitability measure that incorporates arbitrary allocations but which does not include a share of all indirect costs. For example, some organisations falling within this category excluded marketing costs, or non-manufacturing cost,

---

3 The respondents were also given the opportunity to incorporate other chosen measures if they did not conform to the measures in our list.

but included other arbitrary allocations within their profitability measure. Row 4 is self-explanatory. When rows 3 and 4 are merged it can be seen that there is approximately a 50/50 split between the use of contribution and a profitability measure that incorporates overhead allocations. Only 6 per cent of the responding organisations used a profitability measure consisting of contribution less indirect costs assigned using cause-and-effect cost drivers.

The final column of Table 7.6 merits some explanation. This column is an analysis of those respondents who indicated that they used only a single profitability measure and which may thus be of particular interest. These responses are also included in the first column (i.e. the most important measure), but this column includes the replies of those respondents that use either two measures or a single measure. Table 7.6 indicates that 38 per cent of the respondents (*N* = 71) rely only on a single profitability measure. Of these respondents 43 per cent (*N* = 30) use a contribution measure that ignores indirect costs and a further 44 per cent (*N* = 31) rely solely on a profitability measure that incorporates arbitrary cost allocations. Relying only on these approaches is questionable. Our findings therefore suggest that a significant minority of respondents, 61 out of a total of 187 responses (33 per cent), run the risk of using naive information for decision-making. It is also apparent from Table 7.6 that the often quoted view that full/absorption costs are the norm may be overstated.

Table 7.6 Importance of profitability analysis measures for decision-making

	% Indicating most important measure (*N* = 187)	*% Indicating second most important measure* (*N* = 187)	*% Selecting a single measure* (*N* = 71)
1 Revenues less direct or variable costs (contribution)	50	26	43
2 Contribution less indirect costs assigned using cause-and-effect cost drivers	6	7	7
3 Row 2 less arbitrary allocations	11	7	16
4 Bottom-line net profit (sales less all costs)	30	19	28
5 Items inserted by respondents	3	3	6
6 Only a single measure used		38 (*N* = 71)	
	100	100	100

7.7 Information included in the special studies

As indicated earlier, the majority of respondents used profitability analysis as an attention-directing mechanism for signalling the need for more detailed studies. One of the objectives of the research is to ascertain the nature and content of the detailed (special) studies. The following question was therefore asked:

> Where profitability analysis is used as an attention-directing mechanism for signalling the need a more detailed appraisal, please briefly describe the content of the information that is included in the appraisal.

The following statements represent a random sample of 22 replies:[4]

- profit is continually analysed;
- analysis of the standard bill of materials;
- relationship with other products within the portfolio (two comments);
- shareholder value, return on assets, cash flows;
- return on capital employed (two comments) ;
- sales/market trends, cost considerations;
- internal rate of return calculation and the impact of disposal costs;
- indirect costs considered at this stage (the responding unit used contribution for profitability analysis);
- level of central cost allocation;
- market intelligence and future demand volumes;
- product marginal costing;
- review of product components, direct costs and overhead levels;
- appraisal based on a simple ABC model using a spreadsheet (the respondent indicated that ABC was not used for periodic profitability analysis);
- market share analysis, marginal cost analysis, historical sales volumes/prices, future cost trend analysis;
- more detailed analysis of direct relevant costs;
- customer- and product-specific detail with as much specific costs that are known replacing previous apportionments;
- start with base cost and then show what incremental savings would be made each time a specific action is undertaken;
- the associated overheads/fixed costs and whether these can be recovered by a more profitable product being made using the freed capacity.

Approximately half of the above responses seem to be suggesting that an attempt is made to isolate incremental (avoidable) costs when undertaking the more detailed appraisal. Such responses imply that focusing on a profitability measure that includes arbitrary allocations of unavoidable costs for attention-directing may not be accompanied by the use of arbitrary allocations within the special studies. However, it is clear from examining the replies that postal questionnaires are not an ideal mechanism for ascertaining the nature, content and role of special studies. More in-depth interviews or case studies are required for this purpose. A list of all the responses relating to the content of the information that is included in the special studies is presented in Appendix III.

---

4 4 out of the 22 random responses selected did not answer this question.

7.8 Accuracy of observed cost systems

If cost systems fail to capture with sufficient accuracy the resources consumed by cost objects, distorted costs will be reported and there is a danger that potential unprofitable activities will not be highlighted for special studies or that resources will be wasted investigating profitable activities that have been reported as unprofitable within the periodic profitability analysis.

Within the profitability analysis section of the questionnaire, questions were included that focused on the accuracy of assigning indirect costs to cost objects. It was pointed out that these questions related specifically to cost information that is incorporated into the profitability analysis. The findings relating to the number of cost pools and second-stage cost drivers used are reported in Tables 7.7–7.9. Cooper (1988b) has shown how increasing the number of cost pools and/or cost drivers increases the accuracy of the reported product costs. It can be seen from Table 7.7 that 3 per cent of the responding organisations used a single cost pool (i.e. a plant-wide or blanket overhead rate), 14 per cent used fewer than 5 cost pools and 36 per cent used more than 20 cost pools. The reported findings relating to the use of a single cost pool are much lower than the findings reported earlier in the paper for the UK and the USA. They are more consistent with the findings reported by the Scandinavian studies. One possible reason explaining the differences reported in this study and the earlier UK/US studies may relate to the period between the studies. In the intervening years the criticisms of traditional cost systems have been widely publicised and there have been significant improvements in information technology. In addition, the survey sought to include only organisations with established cost systems, and therefore organisations with very simplistic cost systems that use plant-wide rates may have been excluded from the sample. These factors may explain the apparent improvement in traditional cost systems arising from a decline in the use of plant-wide rates.

Table 7.7 Number of cost pools each having their own individual charge-out rate (analysed by cost objects)

	Number of cost pools							
	1	*2–3*	*4–5*	*6–10*	*11–20*	*21–30*	*31–50*	*Over 50*
	%	%	%	%	%	%	%	%
Products/services (*N* = 139)	3	1	6	22	30	12	9	17
Customers (*N* = 8)			25	13	12	25	12	13
Locations (*N* = 14)	7		29	7	29	14	7	7
Other (*N* = 8)		13	12	25	38	12		
Total (*N* = 169)	3	2	9	21	29	13	8	15

Table 7.8 Number of second-stage cost drivers used to assign overheads to cost objects

	Number of cost drivers							
	1	2	3	4	5	6	7–10	Over 10
	%	%	%	%	%	%	%	%
Products/services (*N* = 139)	35	25	11	8	6	1	6	8
Customers (*N* = 8)	13	12	13		12	13		37
Locations (*N* = 14)	36	29	7	7	7			14
Other (*N* = 8)	50	25		25				
Total (*N* = 169)	34	25	10	8	6	2	5	10

Table 7.9 Cross-tabulation table (cost pools by cost drivers)

	Number of cost drivers							
	1	*2*	*3*	*4*	*5*	*6*	*7–10*	*Over 10*
	N %[a]	N %	N %	N %	N %	N %	N %	N %
1 cost pool (*N* = 5)	5 (3)							
2–3 cost pools (*N* = 3)	1 (1)	2 (1)						
4–5 cost pools (*N* = 16)	7 (4)	3 (2)	3 (2)	1 (1)	2 (1)			
6–10 cost pools (*N* = 35)	17 (10)	12 (7)	3 (2)	3 (2)				
11–20 cost pools (*N* = 49)	16 (9)	14 (8)	5 (3)	5 (3)	4 (2)		3 (2)	2 (1)
21–30 cost pools (*N* = 22)	6 (3)	7 (4)	2 (1)		1 (1)	3 (2)		3 (2)
31–50 cost pools (*N* = 14)	4 (2)	2 (1)	2 (1)	3 (2)	1 (1)		1 (1)	1 (1)
Over 50 cost pools (*N* = 25)	2 (1)	2 (1)	2 (1)	2 (1)	2 (1)		5 (3)	10 (6)
Total (*N* = 169)	58 (34)	42 (25)	17 (10)	14 (8)	10 (6)	3 (2)	9 (5)	16 (10)

[a] The numbers in parentheses relate to the number of individual observations *(N)* expressed as a percentage of the total number of observations.

Even if many cost pools are used, indirect costs assigned to cost objects can still be inaccurate if, as Kaplan and Cooper (1998, p. 15) point out, a limited number of second-stage drivers are used. Table 7.8 indicates that a single second-stage cost driver was used by 34 per cent of the organisations and 69 per cent used fewer than 4 cost drivers.[5] More than 10 different types of cost drivers were used by 10 per cent of the organisations. Table 7.9 shows a cross-tabulation table for the number of cost pools by number of second-stage cost drivers used. Only 20 out of the 169 respondents (12 per cent) indicated that their cost system incorporated more than 20 cost pools and more than 6 different cost drivers. An initial observation of Table 7.9 suggests that many organisations are using cost systems that may not accurately assign indirect costs to cost objects. The problem appears to arise because of the use of a limited number of second-stage cost drivers rather than using a limited number of cost pools. However, it is inappropriate to conclude that organisations have inaccurate cost systems without considering potential explanatory factors. For example, unsophisticated systems will not result in the reporting of inaccurate costs in those organisations where indirect costs represent a small proportion of total costs.

7.9 Treatment of facility-sustaining costs

Many resources are acquired in lumpy amounts and decisions resulting in changes in resource usage should be reflected in future changes in the spending on the supply of resources. However, with facility-sustaining costs the resources supplied cover a wide range of activity usage and there would have to be a dramatic change in activity before a decision would be made to change the supply of resources. Hence, facility-sustaining costs tend to remain unchanged, and therefore irrelevant, for most decisions arising from a periodic profitability analysis (e.g. product mix or abandonment

5 By number of cost drivers we mean the number of separate types of cost drivers used. For example, an organisation using 50 cost pools that uses direct labour as the cost driver for each cost pool would be described as using only one type of cost driver.

decisions). However, stock valuation requirements require that manufacturing facility-sustaining costs are assigned to products for inventory valuation. Furthermore, when making pricing or tendering decisions, managers may demand full cost information as a mechanism for seeking to ensure that products/services recover the cost of resources consumed (including facility-sustaining costs). Where costs are used as an input to setting selling prices, the cost system ought to be able to provide a reasonably accurate estimation of facility-sustaining resources consumed by cost objects rather than cost assignment being based on arbitrarily allocations.

One of the respondents drew our attention, in a telephone interview, to the importance for the need for his organisation to accurately assign facility-sustaining costs to customers. A facility was used by different external users, usage varied and not all users used the facility Most of the costs were facility-sustaining and were recharged to users on the basis of an appropriate cost driver. It was considered essential to assign such costs to customers for product pricing and also to avoid arbitrary allocations. To meet these requirements the organisation implemented ABC.

Because the treatment of facility-sustaining costs is likely to be dependent on the purpose for which the information is required, we asked the respondents to indicate how facility-sustaining costs were dealt with and also whether they are categorised separately. If facility-sustaining costs are allocated to cost pools within the first stage of the two-stage allocation procedure, there is a danger that they will be hidden within other costs when cost driver rates are established. Therefore it is unlikely that the costs will be treated differently for different purposes, and also the resulting cost driver rate will suggest an inappropriate degree of variability in respect of the facility-sustaining element of the costs. Most of the respondents (83 per cent) stated that facility-sustaining costs were allocated to cost pools and included within the cost pool overhead target rate, but 78 per cent of these respondents specified that facility-sustaining costs were categorised separately when extracting information for decision-making. The potential therefore exists for facility-sustaining costs to be treated differently for different purposes.

These findings thus provide further evidence to suggest that arbitrary allocations of unavoidable fixed costs may not be used for certain decisions, even when some form of full costs are accumulated within the cost system. The responses suggest that the cost accumulation systems of the majority of the surveyed organisations generate information that provides the potential for cost information to be used in a flexible manner. However, given the findings reported in the previous section, there is a danger that cost systems in many organisations may not accurately measure the facility-sustaining costs consumed by cost objects when costs are used as an input to pricing decisions.

7.10 Extent of ABC usage

It can be seen from Table 7.10 that 15 per cent of the organisations had implemented a full ABC system, 5 per cent indicated partial implementation and a further 3 per cent were actually in the process of implementing it. Those respondents indicating partial implementation specifically volunteered the information. The questionnaire did not provide for a partial implementation response. It is apparent from Table 7.10 that a significantly higher proportion of service and financial and commercial organisations have implemented ABC.[6]

Table 7.10 ABC implementation

	Full implementation %	*Partial implementation* %	*Implementation in progress* %	*No implementation* %
Manufacturing (*N* = 127)	5	7	3	85
Retail (*N* = 10)	20			80
Service (*N* = 27)	34		7	59
Financial and commercial (*N* = 14)	57	7	7	29
Other (*N* = 7)	14			86
Total (*N* = 185)	15	5	3	77

Our telephone conversations with respondents from the financial and commercial sector indicated that many of the organisations within this sector had only begun to implement management accounting within the last decade. Faced with deregulation and a more competitive market, they invested heavily in the management accounting function and committed resources to implementing ABC. The recent establishment of management accounting systems within organisations appears to have a significant influence on the adoption of ABC.

The results reported in Table 7.10 suggest low ABC adoption rates. However, when the responses are analysed by the size of the business organisation, a different picture emerges. Most of the full ABC adopters (85 per cent) were in the largest size category (annual sales turnover in excess of £300m). An analysis of ABC usage for those organisations within the largest size category indicated that 33 per cent were full adopters, 9 per cent were partial adopters and 3 per cent were in the process of implementing ABC. Adding the three categories together, 45 per cent were ABC adopters. Further analysis indicated that there was a statistically significant difference in terms of the size of organisations for ABC adopters and non-adopters.[7]

6 Classifying full, partial and ABC in process of implementation as ABC adopters and the remaining respondents as non-adopters, and classifying business sectors as manufacturing, financial and service, and retail and others, the chi-square (χ^2) test rejected the null hypothesis that there was no association between business type and the adoption of ABC at the 1 per cent level.

7 Both the parametric t-test and the non-parametric Mann–Whitney U-test rejected the null hypothesis that there is no difference in size between ABC adopters and non-adopters at the 1 per cent level.

In terms of ABC applications the responses from the full adopters indicated that:

- 40 per cent used ABC to assign costs to cost objects for generating routine decision-making information;
- 11 per cent used ABC to cost activities for cost management but did not extend it to assigning costs for decision-making;
- 44 per cent used ABC for both cost management and decision-making purposes;
- 5 per cent indicated that an activity analysis was undertaken but the activities were not costed.

Apart from one organisation, all of the manufacturing organisations that were ABC full adopters used their ABC system to assign costs for stock valuation.

It was pointed out in Chapter 5 that in some situations it can be difficult to distinguish an ABC system from a non-ABC system. In order to gain some insight as to what the observed ABC systems consisted of, we analysed the responses of those respondents who had indicated that their organisations were ABC users (i.e. full adopters) by the number of cost pools and the number of different cost driver rates. The analysis revealed the following:

- 50 per cent used more than 10 separate types of cost driver rates;
- 27 per cent used between 7 and 10 separate types of cost driver rates;
- 23 per cent used between 4 and 6 separate types of cost driver rates.

In terms of the number of cost pools we observed the following:

- 50 per cent used more than 50 cost pools;
- 27 per cent used between 21 and 50 cost pools;
- 23 per cent used between 11 and 20 cost pools.

The above analysis suggests that those respondents that claim that their organisations have implemented ABC 'really' are ABC adopters. Even the use of 4 or 5 cost drivers does imply that organisations have moved beyond traditional product-volume-related cost systems.

Further analysis indicated that the cost systems for ABC users contained significantly more cost pools and different types of cost drivers when compared with non-ABC users.[8] A further distinguishing feature of ABC systems is apparent from examining Table 7.9. This table shows that 28 respondents used more than 5 separate cost drivers and 10 cost pools. An analysis of these responses indicated that 26 were ABC adopters. However, the number of cost drivers and cost pools used by a

8 The results were significant at the 1 per cent level using both the parametric t-test and the non-parametric Mann–Whitney U-test.

significant proportion of ABC users would appear to be less than that envisaged by Kaplan and Cooper (1998, p. 102). They suggest that relatively simple ABC systems having 30–50 cost pools and many cost drivers ought to report reasonably accurate costs.

In the Norwegian study, Bjornenak (1997a) reported that for ABC adopters the mean number of cost pools and allocation bases were 30.15 and 1.92 respectively. However, his definition of ABC adopters included organisations that had implemented, were currently implementing or wishing to implement ABC, whereas our findings reported above relate to full implementers of ABC. Therefore the observations are not directly comparable with our study.

7.11 Analysis of profitability by product lines and individual products

In a study of Japanese organisations, Cooper (1996) observed how the low level of customer loyalty had a powerful effect on the way firms competed. First, the firms must be technologically up to date, and second, they must essentially provide a full product line. Cooper states:

> By designing a complete product line, the firm gave the customer minimum reason to look at a competitive offering. If a gap in the line exists so that the customer cannot find the product he wishes, he will go elsewhere.... Consequently most firms believe it to be unacceptable to leave 'a hole in the line'. (p. 221)

Given this strategy, many Japanese firms did not consider product-mix decisions to be particularly important at the individual product level. All significant decisions were made at the product line level. Because of this some of the firms studied implemented cost systems that could only report product line costs.

In terms of this survey, individual products, services or customers were grouped together and categorised as product lines by 89 per cent of the respondents (*N* = 144) and the remaining 11 per cent (*N* = 18) did not categorise their activities by product lines. Of those respondents using product lines, 59 per cent routinely analysed profits only at the product line level and the remaining 41 per cent analysed profits by individual products within the line. However, 78 per cent of those respondents routinely analysing profitability at the product line level indicated that individual product, service or customer service costs could be extracted from the database when required to analyse product line profitability at the individual product level. The cost system for the remaining 22 per cent (*N* = 19) did not accumulate costs by individual items. Therefore profitability could only be ascertained at the product/customer line level. In other words, of the 144 respondents categorising their activities by product/customer lines, only 19 (13 per cent) could not analyse profitability by individual items within the line.

In order to ascertain whether organisations were likely to be adopting a hierarchical approach to profitability analysis similar to the approach described in Chapter 3, those respondents ($N = 59$) that specified that their organisations routinely analysed profits by items within the product or customer line were asked how joint costs were recorded within the profitability analysis. Joint costs that were attributable to the whole product/customer line, and which could thus be directly traced only to the line and not to the individual items within the line, were not allocated to individual items by 52 per cent of the respondents. Instead, they were directly charged as a lump sum against the aggregate contributions arising from all the items within the line. The remaining 48 per cent allocated the joint costs to the individual items within the line using arbitrary allocations.

Table 7.11 Allocation of product line joint costs analysed by percentage of items discontinued in a typical year

	Less than 4% of items discontinued %	*4–7% of items discontinued* %	*More than 7% of items discontinued* %
Joint costs not allocated to items within the line (i.e. traced directly to the line)	47	32	21
Joint cost allocated to items within the line	74	19	7

The responses as to whether profits were analysed by product/customer lines or by individual items within the line were compared using many different potential variables. One might expect ABC adopters to be more interested in individual product profitability than non-adopters, because it is at this level that high- and low-volume products (i.e. volume diversity) would be distinguished. No significant differences between ABC adopters and non-adopters were observed in the analysis of profitability at the individual product or product line level. Only size was significant, with 70 per cent of organisations with an annual sales turnover in excess of £100m, compared with 45 per cent for organisations with a sales turnover of less than £100m, routinely analysing profits at the product/customer line level and not extending the analysis to items within the line.[9] In terms of whether joint costs were assigned to items within the line, the only significant observation was the percentage of items discontinued over a typical year.[10] The observations are reported in Table 7.11. The allocation of joint costs to items within the line appears to be associated with a smaller percentage of items being discontinued over a typical year.

9 Significant at the 5 per cent level using a one-tailed parametric t-test and the non-parametric Mann–Whitney U-test.

10 Significant at the 5 per cent level using a one-tailed parametric t-test and the non-parametric Mann–Whitney U-test.

8

Survey Findings Relating to Cost Information for Stock Valuation and Pricing Decisions and the Activity Levels used for Cost Assignment

8.1 Cost accumulation for stock valuation

8.1.1 Use of separate databases for stock valuation and decision-making

One of the objectives of the research project was to ascertain whether the cost accumulation system adopted by organisations was influenced by the purpose for which the information is required. In particular, the research sought to ascertain whether a more simplistic accumulation system was used for stock valuation when compared with the system used for profitability analysis. We therefore included a separate section in the questionnaire that concentrated solely on stock valuation. The respondents were asked to confirm whether the answers relating to the methods of assigning costs to cost objects within the profitability analysis section also applied to stock valuation. In other words, was the same cost accumulation system used for stock valuation as that used to generate profitability analysis information? Where a separate system was used for stock valuation the respondents were asked to answer additional questions about their cost system.

Only 9 per cent of the manufacturing organisations (twelve respondents) that assigned costs for stock valuation used a separate cost accumulation system, one for stock valuation and the other for profitability analysis. Three of these organisations only assigned direct costs for profitability analysis and indirect costs were assigned to meet stock valuation requirements. Eight organisations stated that they used a more simplistic and less sophisticated system for stock valuation. Of these eight organisations, seven used five or more different cost drivers for accumulating costs for profitability analysis and five were also either partial or full ABC adopters. The remaining organisation used a very simplistic and arbitrary method of allocations within the profitability analysis, because direct costs were the dominant costs and most of the indirect costs were infrastructure costs and unavoidable. Nevertheless, indirect costs were assigned, but the respondent claimed they did not distort the analysis because they were identifiable within the analysis. For stock valuation, a slightly more sophisticated system was used.

Within the stock valuation section of the questionnaire the respondents were also asked to provide information on stock valuations as a percentage of sales to ascertain its relative importance. The results are reported in Table 8.1 for (a) those organisations that used the same cost accumulation system for profitability analysis and stock valuation, and (b) for those that use separate accumulation systems for these purposes. It can be seen that the organisations using separate systems had a lower mean score compared with those organisations using the same accumulation system for both purposes.[1] This may reflect the fact that stock valuation is of a relatively lower value for the organisations in the former category and, to reflect this, more simplistic systems were used for stock valuation.

Table 8.1 Value of stocks as a percentage of annual sales turnover

	N	*Mean*[a]	*Standard deviation*[a]
Same accumulation system used for stock valuation and profitability analysis	124	3.73	1.86
Different accumulation system used for stock valuation and profitability analysis[b]	14	2.71	1.59

[a] A 7-point scale was used, with each point representing an interval of 4 percentage points (i.e. 2 = 5–9%, 3 = 10–14%, 4 = 15–19%).
[b] Includes two non-manufacturing organisations classified within the 'Other' category in Table 7.2.

8.1.2 Influence of financial accounting

In section 4.4 the claim that management accounting information is extracted from accounting systems that are designed primarily for meeting financial accounting requirements was discussed. It was pointed out that, if companies use a single database that contains information derived from an unsophisticated cost system, or the database is not designed to enable the cost information to be extracted in a flexible manner for decision-making, the claim that financial accounting dominates management accounting cannot be rejected.

We examined the replies from all those organisations that indicated that costs were accumulated for inventory valuation and their value was significant for financial reporting. The analysis indicated that 24 per cent of the organisations used unsophisticated systems, 67 per cent used systems of a low sophistication level and 9 per cent used sophisticated systems (see section 9.2 for an explanation of how the sophistication levels were derived). The analysis also indicated that 53 per cent of the organisations could not distinguish between cause-and-effect and arbitrary cost allocations. In other words, cost information could not be extracted from the database in a flexible manner. These findings suggest that, for the majority of those organisations where

1 The results were significant at the 5 per cent two-tailed level using the Mann–Whitney U-test.

inventory valuation was significant for financial reporting, the claim that financial accounting dominates management accounting cannot be rejected.

8.1.3 Respondents' views on the accuracy of the cost systems

The respondents were also asked a question on a 7-point scale relating to their views on the accuracy of their organisation's cost system for stock valuation. The mean score on a scale of 1 (not very accurate) to 7 (extremely accurate) was 4.29 ($\sigma = 1.33$). A similar question was also asked for information derived from profitability analysis for decision-making (mean = 3.83, $\sigma = 1.43$). Further analysis indicated that 28 per cent of the respondents for stock valuation, and 43 per cent for decision-making, inserted a score of 3 or less. The responses suggest that a significant number of respondents consider that their cost systems are not particularly accurate for decision-making. This finding is consistent with our earlier findings in section 7.8 relating to the inaccuracy of the observed cost systems in a significant number of organisations. Table 8.2 reports the results for those respondents who used the same cost accumulation system for stock valuation and profitability analysis. The results suggest that, because less accurate cost are likely to suffice for stock valuation, the respondents viewed the cost accumulation systems as being more accurate for meeting stock valuation requirements.[2]

Table 8.2 Respondents' views on the accuracy of the cost systems

	N	*Mean*[a]	*Standard deviation*	*% Rating 1 or 2*	*% Rating 6 or 7*
Rating for accuracy for profitability analysis	116	3.74	1.45	21.6	11.2
Rating for stock valuation	116	4.29	1.29	11.3	15.3

[a] The respondents were asked to indicate their views by recording a score on a scale from 1 (not very accurate) to 7 (extremely accurate).

8.2 Cost information for setting selling prices

8.2.1 Use of a separate database for cost-plus pricing

A separate section in the questionnaire was devoted to the cost accumulation system that was used and the information that was extracted for cost-plus pricing. Sixty per cent of the respondents indicated that cost-plus pricing was used to assist in setting selling prices. The discussion that follows relates only to the replies from these respondents.

One of the objectives of the research was to ascertain whether a separate cost accumulation system was maintained when cost-plus pricing was extensively used. We also sought to ascertain whether organisations for which a significant part of their business involves using cost data for bidding/pricing are more likely to develop sophisticated cost systems, since undercosting is likely to lead to the acceptance of unprofitable business whereas overcosting may lead to the loss of profitable business.

2 The results were significant at the 1 per cent two-tailed level using the Wilcoxon matched-pairs test.

Based on the notion of different costs for different purposes, we asked the respondents to specify the cost accumulation system that was used for setting selling prices. They were asked to specify which of the following statements applied:

1 The earlier responses relating to the profitability analysis system correctly describe the system for accumulating costs for cost-plus pricing.
2 The earlier responses for stock valuation correctly describe the system for accumulating costs for cost-plus pricing.
3 Responses 1 and 2 do not apply.

If the respondents specified item 3 above, they were asked to complete questions relating to the cost accumulation system specifically used for pricing decisions. Of those respondents that used costs as an aid to setting selling prices, 98 per cent ticked the first response above, 2 per cent ticked the second response and none of the respondents specified the third response. It appears that organisations do not maintain different cost systems for pricing decisions.

8.2.2 Information extracted from the database for cost-plus pricing

Even though separate cost systems are not used for cost-plus pricing, different information may be extracted from the database for pricing decisions. The analysis of the responses relating to the cost information that was used for cost-plus pricing indicated that :

- 15 per cent assigned only direct costs to cost objects for cost-plus pricing (this included 9 per cent that assigned only direct variable costs and a further 6 per cent that assigned both direct variable and non-variable costs);
- 7 per cent assigned direct costs plus those indirect costs where cost drivers could be identified that are the causes of the cost varying in the long term;
- 78 per cent assigned direct costs plus those indirect costs identified in the second category above, plus a share of those costs (e.g. infrastructure costs) that are assigned using methods that do not rely on cause-and-effect allocations.

The above results are significantly different from those reported in Table 7.6 which relates to profitability analysis information that is used for discontinuation, redesign and outsourcing decisions.[3] Table 7.6 suggests a greater usage of a direct costing approach, with 50 per cent of the responding organisations identifying contribution (sales revenues less direct costs) as the most important measure for profitability analysis compared with 15 per cent, described above, that assign only direct costs for cost-plus pricing. A comparison of the above responses shown in the third category above

---

3 Table 7.6 incorporates responses for all organisations, whereas for comparison purposes it should incorporate only organisations that use cost-plus pricing. The results and percentages reported are virtually identical to those reported in Table 7.6 if those organisations only using cost-plus pricing are included in the analysis.

with those in Table 7.6 also suggests that some form of full costs are more widely used for pricing decisions. It can be seen that 78 per cent used a full cost approach for pricing decisions compared with 41 per cent which indicated that such costs were incorporated within the most important profitability measure for decision-making.

8.2.3 Importance of derived cost-plus prices in determining selling prices

We also asked questions relating to the extent of the usage and importance of cost-plus pricing for sales to external customers. Cost-plus pricing was used by 60 per cent of the responding organisations. For those organisations that used cost-plus pricing, it accounted for over 40 per cent of total sales revenue in 44 per cent of the organisations and less than 10 per cent in 26 per cent of the organisations.

In terms of importance in determining the final selling price a 7-point scale was used, ranging from 1 (of little importance) to 7 (of vital importance). The average score was 4.54 (standard deviation = 1.70), with 33 per cent of the respondents entering a score of greater than 5. The responses were analysed by the extent of cost-plus pricing (measured by the sales revenue derived from cost-plus pricing expressed as a percentage of total sales revenues). The results are reported in Table 8.3. As may be expected, the importance of the derived cost-plus price in determining the final selling price appears to be positively related to the extent to which cost-plus pricing is used.[4]

Table 8.3 Respondents' views on the importance of the derived cost-plus price in determining the final selling price

% of sales revenues accounted for by cost-plus pricing	*N*	*Mean[a]*	*Standard deviation*	*% Rating 1 or 2*	*% Rating 6 or 7*
1–20%	47	3.60	1.46	25	13
21%–50%	19	4.79	1.81	10	42
Over 50%	42	5.50	1.25	5	52

[a] The respondents were asked to indicate their views by recording a score on a scale from 1 (of little importance) to 7 (of vital importance).

The responses for those organisations that used cost-plus pricing extensively (i.e. sales revenues from cost-plus pricing accounted for more than 40 per cent of total sales revenues) were examined, but no evidence was found to indicate that they used a different number of cost pools or cost drivers.

4 The Spearman rank correlation coefficient was 0.52 ($p < 0.01$ two-tailed) and the observations reported in Table 8.3 were significant at the 1 per cent level using the Kruskal–Wallis non-parametric test.

8.3 Defining activity levels for cost assignment

8.3.1 Alternative measures of activity levels

Organisations assigning indirect costs to cost objects must decide on the denominator activity level to be used in order to establish cost centre or activity centre cost driver (overhead absorption) rates. Activity volume levels can be measured in a number of different ways and the actual method selected can have a profound effect on the costs that are assigned to cost objects and unutilised capacity. Three different activity measures are discussed in the literature:

1. Normal volume based on the anticipated average level of activity that will satisfy average customer demand over a period of years, e.g. 3–5 years (6 per cent).
2. Budgeted or estimated annual activity (90 per cent).
3. Maximum practical annual capacity that is available – this is the capacity that is expected to be available for the period and includes both planned utilised and unutilised capacity (4 per cent).

The numbers in parentheses for each of the three methods listed above represent the percentage of respondents using each method.[5] The emergence of ABC as a resource consumption model is based on the assumption that ABC systems assign the cost of resources used to cost objects, and the difference between the cost of resources supplied and the cost of resources used represents the cost of unused capacity. In order to measure the cost of used and unused capacity, ABC theory is based on the assumption that practical capacity should be used as the denominator level for determining cost driver rates. The justification for using practical capacity was presented in Chapter 3.

8.3.2 Justification for using practical capacity

In Chapter 3 it was pointed out that practical capacity is most suited to measuring human resources, but it is more problematic when physical resources are measured. Because of this, some textbooks (e.g. Drury, 1996) argue that normal volume should be used to measure physical resources. The justification for using this measure is that it provides an approximation of the long-run average costs of providing a firm's operating capacity, since seasonal and cyclical variations and trend factors are averaged out. In particular, the proponents of this method argue that stable long-run average cost driver rates are more meaningful than rates that fluctuate from year to year. In many situations, however, distinguishing between normal volume and practical capacity will only become an important issue when normal volume is substantially below practical capacity.

Most textbooks reject the use of annual budgeted activity (e.g. Drury, 1996, p. 95; Kaplan and Cooper, 1998, p. 116). This is because the cost driver rate will fluctuate from year to year and this can lead to the reporting of distorted costs and

5 The total number of responses relating to the activity measure used was $N = 159$.

incorrect decisions. For example, in a recession annual budgeted activity will be declining, but if capacity is maintained in the expectation that there will be a resurgence in demand, capacity costs will remain unchanged and cost driver rates will increase. In these circumstances the application of a cost-based pricing formula will suggest a price increase at the very worst time – when business is slack. A price increase might further reduce demand and trigger another increase in the cost driver rate and thereby prompt a further price increase. Cooper and Kaplan describe companies that use annual budgeted activity as running the risk of triggering off a 'death spiral'.

8.3.3 Widespread use of annual budgeted activity

Most of the respondents (90 per cent) used annual budgeted activity as the denominator level. However, if, during the annual budgeting process, organisations adjust the capacity supplied (practical capacity) towards the level of budgeted activity, the choice of activity denominator level is unlikely to result in the computation of significantly different cost driver rates and, therefore, the reported costs assigned to cost objects and unused capacity. An analysis of those organisations that did not use annual budgeted activity did not identify any distinguishing features that would explain why their responses differed from the rest of the respondents. The responses for the ABC adopters were analysed, but their responses were virtually identical to the non-ABC adopters. Overall, the findings suggest a possible significant difference between theory and practice, and the rationale justifying the choice of activity denominator levels would appear to be an area requiring further research.

The respondents were also asked whether their organisations measured the cost of unused capacity for cost centres/pools. The responses were 20 per cent for 'Yes' and 80 per cent for 'No'. It is possible that some of the respondents measure unused capacity in physical terms but not in monetary terms. The replies were examined for potential explanatory factors, such as size and ABC usage, but none could be found.

9

Survey Findings Relating to the Influence of Potential Explanatory Variables on Cost System Design and the Information Extracted from the System

9.1 Different cost accumulation systems for different purposes

In Chapter 5 we divided cost accumulation systems into four different categories and suggested that the choice of the cost accumulation system depended on the purpose for which the information was required. The survey findings indicated that 93 per cent of the organisations maintained a single database from which appropriate cost information was extracted to provide the required information for stock valuation, periodic profitability analysis and pricing decisions. Only 9 per cent ($N = 12$) of those manufacturing organisations that assigned costs for stock valuation maintained a separate database for stock valuation and decision-making. There were no observable explanatory factors that distinguished these twelve organisations from those that maintained a single database. The findings therefore do not support the hypothesis that the purpose for which the cost information is required influences the type of cost accumulation system.

However, different information appears to be extracted from the cost system depending on the purpose for which the information is required. In terms of the most important profitability measure that was used for decision-making (excluding setting selling prices), Table 9.1 indicates that there is approximately a 50/50 split between the use of a contribution measure (sales less direct or variable costs) and a profitability measure that incorporates indirect cost allocations. In contrast, only 15 per cent used direct costs for cost-plus pricing and the remainder used costs that incorporated indirect cost allocations.

Table 9.1 Information extracted from the cost system for different decision-making requirements

	Cost-plus pricing decisions	*Other decisions*[a]
	%	%
Direct or variable costs	15	50
Some form of full costs	85	47
Other		3
	100	100

[a] Other decisions relate to the costs incorporated in the profitability measures that the respondents focused on for signalling the need to make discontinuation, redesign or outsourcing decisions.

9.2 Level of sophistication and accuracy in assigning costs to cost objects

A major objective of the research was to investigate whether potential explanatory factors influenced the level of sophistication of the cost system in assigning indirect costs to cost objects. The level of sophistication cannot be directly observed or measured. Therefore a proxy measure of sophistication was established. Table 7.9 (the cross-tabulation table reporting the combination of the number of cost pools with the number of different second-stage drivers) was used to identify the following three different categories of sophistication:

Category 1: Unsophisticated systems.
Category 2: Systems of a low sophistication level.
Category 3: Sophisticated systems.

The first category consisted of those organisations with fewer than 5 cost pools and 2 drivers plus those organisations with 6–10 cost pools and only 1 driver. It can be seen from Table 7.9 that adopting this criterion results in 35 organisations (21 per cent) being included in the unsophisticated category. Organisations using more than 10 cost pools and 5 or more cost drivers were assigned to the third category. Therefore, 36 organisations (21 per cent) were included within the sophisticated category (see Table 7.9). The remaining 98 organisations (58 per cent) in Table 7.9 were classified within the second category. It was difficult to develop additional categories, since any further analysis of these 98 organisations by levels of sophistication is problematic.

Because of the reasons explained in Chapter 5 we did not consider whether or not the organisations were ABC users in determining the above classification criteria. An analysis of ABC full-implementation organisations, however, indicated that 7 per cent fell within the second category and 93 per cent within the third category. The respondents were also asked to indicate on a 7-point scale (1 = not very accurate and 7 = extremely accurate) their perceived level of accuracy of their cost systems in assigning indirect costs to cost objects for decision-making. Even the most sophisticated systems are unlikely to be extremely accurate. Therefore modest scores might be assigned to such systems by knowledgeable accountants. Also, some respondents assigned high accuracy scores to what appeared to be very unsophisticated systems.

If indirect costs in the respondents' organisations are relatively small, then a high accuracy score may be justifiable for an unsophisticated system. For these reasons we chose to establish an objective measure of sophistication. However, we conducted statistical tests to test the null hypothesis that there was no association between the respondents' accuracy rating and the three different categories of sophistication. The hypothesis was rejected at the 1 per cent level.[6] These factors suggest that the assignment of the responses into the three categories provides an appropriate basis to measure the level of sophistication of the observed cost systems.

9.3 Impact of potential explanatory factors

The survey findings relating to the relationship between the potential explanatory variables and the three categories of sophistication are shown in Table 9.2.

9.3.1 Competitive environment

Items (a) to (c) in Table 9.2 attempt to measure the competitive environment. For (a) the respondents were asked to indicate on a scale of 1 to 7 (with 1 indicating 'low' and 7 'extremely intensive') the extent of competition for their organisation's major products/services. There is a significant difference between organisations adopting unsophisticated and sophisticated cost systems if the comparison focuses only on these two categories.[7] However, the findings are not significant if a comparison is made between all three categories. It can be seen for all three categories that competition was considered to be intensive.

The second measure used for the competitive environment is predictability of competitors' marketing activities, with the 7-point scale ranging from a score of 1 (becoming more predictable) to 7 (becoming less predictable). The findings suggest that organisations with a lower mean score, and lower percentages with a rating of 6 or 7, are more likely to have unsophisticated cost systems. The differences were significant at the 5 per cent level.[8]

The final measure relating to the competitive environment shown in Table 9.2 (row c) is the intensity of price competition. The 7-point scale ranged from 1 (of negligible intensity) to 7 (extremely intensive). Most of the respondents within each category assigned a score of 6 or 7, the average being approximately 6 for all three categories. Given the clustering of responses, it is not surprising that there is no statistically significant difference in respect of the intensity of price competition within the three sophistication categories.

---

6 The results were significant at the 1 per cent level using the Kruskal–Wallis and chi-square tests. The Spearman rank correlation coefficient was 0.29 ($p = 0.001$) and the Cramer coefficient was 0.33 ($p = 0.001$).

7 Significant at the 5 per cent level using the Mann–Whitney two-tailed U-test.

8 The Kruskal–Wallis one-way Anova test rejected the null hypothesis that there is no difference in the predictability of the competitors' market activities for the organisations within the three sophistication categories.

Table 9.2 Cost system sophistication and potential explanatory variables

	N	Mean	Standard deviation	% rating 1 or 2	% rating 6 or 7
(a) *Extent of competition for major products/services*					
Unsophisticated	35	5.514	1.269	2.9	54.3
Low sophistication	98	5.806	1.181	1.0	65.3
Sophisticated	36	5.971	1.465	5.7	75.0
(b) *Predictability of the activities of competitors*					
Unsophisticated	33	3.970	1.237	9.1	9.1
Low sophistication	95	4.547	1.183	6.3	19.4
Sophisticated	33	4.543	1.146	8.6	14.3
(c) *Intensity of price competition*					
Unsophisticated	35	6.086	0.781	0	80.0
Low sophistication	97	5.959	1.050	1.0	72.2
Sophisticated	36	6.139	1.268	2.8	86.1
(d) *Variation in consumption of support dept costs*					
Unsophisticated	35	3.794	1.629	17.6	20.5
Low sophistication	96	3.917	1.646	22.9	18.7
Sophisticated	33	4.242	1.521	15.2	22.2
(e) *Degree of customisation*					
Unsophisticated	35	3.486	1.805	48.6	17.1
Low sophistication	97	3.278	1.742	45.4	14.4
Sophisticated	36	2.639	1.150	52.8	0
(f) *Volume diversity*					
Unsophisticated	35	5.833	1.704	3.3	66.7
Low sophistication	91	5.868	1.655	5.5	73.6
Sophisticated	30	5.567	1.775	10.0	60.0
(g) *Number of items costed within chosen cost object*	*N*	*0–40*	*41–200*		*Over 200*
Unsophisticated	34	20.6	23.5		55.9
Low sophistication	97	17.5	18.5		64.0
Sophisticated	36	22.2	33.3		44.5
(h) *Size (£m annual sales turnover)*	*N*	*>£100m*	*£100–299m*		*<£300m*
Unsophisticated	35	65.7	22.9		11.4
Low sophistication	97	47.4	24.8		27.8
Sophisticated	36	5.5	16.7		77.8
(i) *Type of business organisation*	*N*	*% Manuf.*	*% Fin. service*		*% Other*
Unsophisticated	35	77.2	11.4		11.4
Low sophistication	98	80.6	11.2		8.2
Sophisticated	36	38.9	52.8		8.3
(j) *Cost structure (as a percentage of total costs)*	*N*	*% Mean (direct)*	*% Mean (indirect)*		*St. dev.*
Unsophisticated	31	66.0	34.0		17.2
Low sophistication	96	70.2	29.8		15.3
Sophisticated	36	68.3	31.7		19.8

9.3.2 Product diversity

Greater product diversity requires more sophisticated cost systems to capture the variation in resource consumption by different products/services. Product diversity can take many different forms. Four measures were used in the survey to measure product diversity. The first (variation in consumption of support department costs) is shown in row (d) of Table 9.2. The respondents were asked to indicate on a 7-point scale (with 1 representing little variation and 7 representing considerable variation) the variation in the consumption of support department resources by the different items within their chosen cost object. The scores were similar for all three categories (and therefore not significant), with the average scores ranging from 3.794 to 4.242.

The degree of customised output of the products/services was the second measure of product diversity used in the survey. For the 7-point rating scale, a score of 1 was labelled 'highly standardised' and a score of 7 'totally customised'. The findings are reported in row (e) of Table 9.2. The average scores for the three categories ranged from 2.6 to 3.5, but the results were not significant at the 5 per cent level.

The third measure (volume diversity) was measured by asking the respondents to indicate on a 7-point scale (with 1 representing little variation and 7 representing considerable variation) how much variation there was in the sales volumes between the top 20 per cent of the best-selling items and the bottom 20 per cent of the lowest-selling items. It is apparent from row (f) of Table 9.2 that there were no significant differences between the categories, with the average scores ranging from 5.567 to 5.868.

The final product diversity measure used was the number of items costed in a typical year within the respondent's chosen cost object. It can be seen from Table 9.2 (row (g)) that in a typical year approximately 80 per cent of the respondents in each category costed more than 40 items. The percentages vary within each category for over 200 items costed, with 64 per cent of the organisations within the low sophistication category and 44.5 per cent within the sophisticated category costing over 200 items. However, the results are not significant, even at the 10 per cent level.

9.3.3 Competitive strategy

The competitive strategy that a firm follows is extremely difficult to measure. We decided not to ask the repondents which of the three competitive strategies (see section 5.3.5) that their organisation pursues because these strategies may not be explicitly stated. Also, top mangement, rather than accountants, are likely to be the most appropriate individuals to derive the information. Instead, we used the measures described for product diversity in the previous section as proxies, for competitive strategies, since product and volume diversity are likely to be associated with firms following a differentiation strategy. Using these proxies, we could not find any evidence to indicate that competitive strategy influenced the sophistication of the observed cost systems.

9.3.4 Size (£m annual turnover)

It can be seen from Table 9.2 (row (h)) that there are significant differences in the size of the organisations within the three sophistication categories.[9] For the unsophisticated cost system category, 65.7 per cent of the organisations had an annual sales turnover of less than £100m, whereas 11.4 per cent had an annual turnover in excess of £300m. In contrast, for the sophisticated cost system category, 5.5 per cent of the organisations had an annual sales turnover below £100m compared with 77.8 per cent for a turnover in excess of £300m.

---

9 The Kruskal–Wallis one-way Anova test rejected the null hypothesis that there is no difference in the size of the organisations within the three sophistication categories at the 1 per cent level.

As well as analysing the sophistication categories by size, we also analysed size by sophistication categories (Table 9.3). For the largest size grouping (over £300m), 48 per cent of the organisations were classified within the sophisticated category and 6 per cent within the unsophisticated category. In contrast, for organisations with less than £100m annual sales turnover, 3 per cent were classified within the sophisticated category and 32 per cent within the unsophisticated category.

Table 9.3 Analysis of annual sales turnover by cost system sophistication categories

	N	*% Unsophisticated*	*% Low sophistication*	*% Sophisticated*
Less than £100m	71	32	65	3
£101–300m	38	21	63	16
Over £300m	59	6	46	48

9.3.5 Type of business organisation

It is also apparent from Table 9.2 (row (i)) that there are significant differences in the types of organisation within the three sophistication categories.[10] For the unsophisticated cost systems category, 77.2 per cent of the organisations were located within the manufacturing sector and 11.4 per cent within the financial and commercial and service sectors. In contrast, within the sophisticated systems category, 38.9 per cent were within the manufacturing sector and 52.8 per cent within the financial/services sector. To provide further insights, a cross-tabulation table is presented in Table 9.4 of the cost sophistication categories for the three business sectors. It can be seen that 22 per cent of the manufacturing organisations were classified within the unsophisticated category and 12 per cent within the sophisticated category, whereas the corresponding observations for the financial and commercial and the service sectors were 12 per cent and 56 per cent.

Table 9.4 Analysis of business sectors by cost sophistication categories

	N	*% Unsophisticated*	*% Low sophistication*	*% Sophisticated*
Manufacturing	120	22	66	12
Financial and service	34	12	32	56
Retail and other	13	27	53	20

It is possible that the above observations may be distorted because of the size impact. For example, if all financial and service organisations are within the largest size category, size may be the major determinant accounting for these organisations having more sophisticated cost systems. We neutralised the size effect by analysing the results for all organisations in the largest size category. The above findings still remain valid, with the observations being similar to those reported in Table 9.4.

10 The chi-square test (χ^2) rejected the null hypothesis at the 1 per cent level that there was no difference in the types of organisations within the three sophistication categories.

9.3.6 Cost structures

The percentage average direct and indirect costs for each cost sophistication category are shown in row (j) of Table 9.2. There are no statistically significant differences in the cost structures between the three categories. The overall average direct and indirect costs for all organisations within the survey that provided details of their cost structures were 69.94 per cent and 30.06 per cent respectively (see Table 7.2). Surprisingly, the average indirect costs were highest for the unsophisticated cost systems category (34.0 per cent). It is suggested that organisations within this category may benefit from improved sophistication, although such a recommendation is moderated by the impact of other explanatory factors. There is, however, a greater variation in the cost structures for the organisations within the sophisticated category.

The results were also analysed after controlling for the size effect, by comparing the cost structures for each of the three sophistication categories for small, medium and large organisations, but no significant differences in the cost structures were observed. We also compared the responses of those organisations whose indirect costs were less than or equal to 15 per cent of total costs ($N = 42$) with those organisations with indirect costs exceeding 50 per cent of total costs ($N = 27$). The distributions by the three sophistication categories were similar for both groupings.

9.3.7 Other observations

Other relationships besides those explicitly defined in the research objectives were examined. There was no association between the importance attached to profitability analysis (i.e. the responses shown in Table 7.5) or the profitability measures used (i.e. the measures listed in Table 7.6) and the different cost systems sophistication categories. Also, there was no evidence to indicate that those organisations that extensively used cost-plus pricing adopted more sophisticated cost systems. Finally, the responses for those organisations that adopted direct or variable costing were compared with those that did not in terms of size, cost structures and the number of items costed. There was no significant relationship between these items and the type of cost system adopted.

10

Conclusions

10.1 Summary of major findings

The major findings were as follows:

- Most organisations routinely analyse profits by their chosen cost objects at monthly intervals.
- Profitability analysis is used as an attention-directing mechanism for identifying potential unprofitable activities that require more detailed studies.
- A single cost system is operated by most organisations.
- The majority of organisations are using relatively unsophisticated cost systems that may not accurately assign indirect costs to cost objects. Such costs may not be sufficiently accurate for providing attention-directing information or information for pricing decisions.
- Most cost systems separately report short-term indirect costs.
- Approximately 80 per cent of the responding firms assigned facility-sustaining (infrastructure) costs, and the norm was to categorise them separately when extracting information for decision-making.
- There was an approximately 50/50 split between the use of a contribution measure (sales less direct or variable costs) and a profitability measure that incorporates indirect cost allocations when interpreting profitability information for attention-directing purposes.
- Cost-plus pricing was used by 60 per cent of the responding firms. Eighty per cent of the responding firms used some form of full (i.e. absorption) costs for cost-plus pricing. Thus full costs were used to a greater extent for cost-plus pricing compared with the profitability analysis information that is used as an attention-directing device.
- Most companies have cost systems that enable them to distinguish between short-term incremental costs and indirect fixed costs, and approximately 50 per cent attempted to distinguish between cause-and-effect and arbitrary allocations of indirect costs. Many companies thus have the potential to use cost information in a flexible manner, and this was evident from the information relating to the responses to the information that was included in special studies.
- There is a relatively low adoption (25 per cent) of ABC systems, but adoption is related to size and business sector. Adoption rates were 45 per cent for the largest firms and 51 per cent for financial and service organisations.
- ABC systems coincide with the more sophisticated systems, as defined in the study.

- A much greater percentage of financial/commercial and service organisations have developed sophisticated cost systems compared with manufacturing organisations.
- Larger organisations tend to have more sophisticated cost systems.
- Approximately 50 per cent of the respondents considered that their cost systems were not particularly accurate for decision-making. However, there was more satisfaction with the accuracy for inventory valuation. This may reflect the fact that, for this purpose, product costs need not be so 'accurate'.
- Activity levels usually relate to budgeted levels for setting cost driver rates, and only 4 per cent of responding organisations had adopted the latest theoretical advice (i.e. to use practical capacity) advocated in the ABC literature.
- Potential explanatory factors were examined to ascertain the extent to which they influenced the sophistication of the observed cost systems. The findings suggest that the competitive environment faced by an organisation, size and the type of business an organisation engages in have a significant influence on the observed cost systems.

10.2 Generalising research findings

Our aim was to concentrate on companies with established cost systems. To achieve this objective we selected a sample consisting of all organisations whose objectives were profit-making and that employed two or more CIMA-qualified members with more than five years' post-qualification experience. This selection process is likely to have resulted in the omission of many small organisations, since they are unlikely to have well-established management accounting systems. Furthermore, many service organisations tend to be relatively small, compared with manufacturing organisations, and many do not have profit-making objectives (e.g. charities and public-sector organisations). Thus our sample contains a lower proportion of service organisations than that which applies for the UK as a whole.

Although our sample does not constitute a representative sample of UK companies, we have sought to justify in section 6.2 that there are strong grounds for believing that it constitutes a representative sample of UK companies with established cost systems. We therefore reiterate the point made in Chapter 6: that is, the findings cannot be generalised to apply to organisations that do not meet the criteria we have used to establish the sample. In particular, care must be exercised in concluding that financial/commercial and service organisations have more sophisticated cost systems than manufacturing organisations. As indicated above, many of the service organisations that do not have established management accounting systems will be excluded from our sample. Our findings do, however, suggest that where financial/commercial and service organisations have established cost systems, they are likely to be more sophisticated than those operated by manufacturing organisations.

10.3 Measurement of explanatory variables and sophistication of the cost systems

A major objective of this study has been to examine the extent to which potential explanatory variables influence the sophistication of the observed cost systems and the information that is extracted from the system. Six potential variables were examined: the purposes for which the cost information is required, cost structures, competitive environment, product diversity, size and type of organisation. Because most organisations used a single cost accumulation system, the findings indicated that the purpose for which the information was required did not influence the choice of the cost accumulation system. However, different cost information appeared to be extracted, depending on the purpose for which the information was required. As indicated above, the findings also suggest that the competitive environment, size and type of business organisation influenced the sophistication of the cost accumulation system. However, there was no evidence to indicate that product diversity or cost structures were explanatory factors.

A major problem is finding appropriate measures for the potential explanatory variables and the sophistication of the cost accumulation systems. For some of the variables, objective measures are not available and proxy measures have to be used. Therefore the observation that no relationship exists between the observed variable and the sophistication of the cost system may be due to the inability to measure the variable or the choice of a poor proxy measure. For example, cost structure was measured by two categories – direct and indirect costs as a percentage of total costs. An ideal measure would extract the percentage of indirect costs that can be more accurately assigned to cost objects using sophisticated cost systems and which fluctuate in the longer term according to the demand for them. Infrastructure costs do not fall within this category and should be distinguished separately from other indirect costs. However, a more detailed analysis of indirect costs is extremely difficult within a large-scale survey and therefore a more simplistic measure of cost structure has been used. It is possible that future research may be able to develop more refined measures to support or refute the results presented in Chapter 9.

The method of assigning cost systems into three sophistication categories may also be questioned. More refined analysis should incorporate the type (e.g. transaction, duration, volume and non-volume) as well as the number of different cost drivers used. An alternative and possibly more objective approach would have been to classify the sophistication of cost systems in terms of ABC and non-ABC systems. We also adopted this approach and virtually all our findings remain unchanged. Cost structure and product diversity were still not significant in distinguishing between ABC and non-ABC adopters.

10.4 Areas for further research

This survey has identified a number of areas that warrant further research. The evidence from the survey suggests that several different categories of costs are separately reported and that the potential exists for cost information to be used in a flexible manner. Future studies should examine in more detail which costs are included within the cost systems, in particular the extent to which manufacturing organisations incorporate non-inventorable costs. The nature, role and content of the cost information that is used, and the role it plays, within special studies is also an area of particular interest for future research. Such insights may be more appropriately determined by case study and interview-based research.

It was also apparent from the survey that the denominator levels used to establish cost driver rates are not consistent with the theoretical approaches advocated by Kaplan and Cooper that underpin modern cost systems. If practical capacity is not used to establish cost driver rates, then the presumption that modern cost systems represent resource consumption models that distinguish between used and unused resources becomes questionable. Future research should investigate why activity levels different from practical capacity are used. The implications of the use of different capacity levels for cost systems, and the use and provision of information to manage the costs of used and unused capacity, should be explored further. Managing the cost of used and unused capacity has been identified as being the central focus of ABC.

It is also apparent from the research that wide differences exist in the sophistication of the observed cost systems. Potential explanatory factors were examined, but there is also a need for case study research to provide a richer insight into explaining why some organisations adopt unsophisticated systems and others do not. For example, one respondent suggested that his organisation had operated for many years in a very favourable economic environment generating high profits, and therefore little attention was given to the cost system, resulting in a very unsophisticated system being used. However, as the economic environment became more hostile and profitability declined, considerably more attention was given to designing and improving the cost system.

One of the practitioner reviewers of this publication pointed out to us that the implementation and development of more sophisticated cost systems is likely to be affected by the extent to which a person who can influence the design and use of the cost system (such as a member of top management, the financial director or the management accountant) has the characteristics of a good champion. He had observed that the presence of a good champion can have as much influence on the design and use of the cost system as the explanatory factors examined in the survey. In terms of the ABC literature, several studies have identified the presence of a good champion and top management support as major factors influencing the implementation and success of ABC systems (e.g. Innes and Mitchell, 1995; Shields, 1995; Foster and Swenson, 1997; Krumweide, 1998). Insights relating to the factors described in this and the preceding paragraph are extremely difficult to derive from research relying solely on postal questionnaire surveys. To complement this study, there is a need for case study research which seeks to identify and ascertain the extent to which other factors not examined in this study influence the design of cost systems.

Finally, the research has concentrated on cost system design and the information generated from the cost system for decisions relating to managing the existing mix of activities, products, services, locations and customers. There is a need for similar research that examines the content of management accounting information, and the role it plays, in managing the cost and mix of future activities.

References

Anthony, R.N. (1989), 'Reminiscences about management accounting', *Journal of Management Accounting Research,* 1 (Fall), pp. 1–20.

Armitage, H.M. and Nicholson, R. (1993), 'Activity-based costing: a survey of Canadian practice', Issue Paper No. 3, Society of Management Accountants of Canada.

Ask, U. and Ax, C. (1992), 'Trends in the Development of Product Costing Practices and Techniques – A Survey of Swedish Manufacturing Industry', *paper presented at the 15th Annual Congress of the European Accounting Association, Madrid, Spain.*

Ask, U., Ax, C. and Jonsson, S. (1996), Cost management in Sweden: from modern to post-modern, in Bhimani, A. (ed) *Management Accounting: European Perspectives,* Oxford: Oxford University Press, pp. 199–217.

Ballas, A. and Venieris, G. (1996), 'A survey of management accounting practices in Greek firms', in Bhimani, A. (ed.), *Management Accounting: European Perspectives,* Oxford: Oxford University Press, pp. 123–39.

Bjornenak, T. (1997a), 'Diffusion and accounting: the case of ABC in Norway', *Management Accounting Research,* Vol. 8, No. 1, pp. 3–17.

Bjornenak, T. (1997b), 'Conventional wisdom and accounting practices', *Management Accounting Research,* Vol. 8, No. 4, pp. 367–82.

Bromwich, M. and Bhimani, A. (1994), *Management Accounting: Pathways to Progress,* London: Chartered Institute of Management Accountants.

Burns, J., Scapens, R. and Turley, S. (1996), 'Some further thoughts on the changing practice of management accounting', *Management Accounting,* October, 58–60.

Chenhall, R.H. and Langfield-Smith, K. (1998), 'Adoption and benefits of management accounting practices: an Australian perspective', *Management Accounting Research,* Vol. 9, No. 1, pp. 1–20.

Clarke, P.J. (1992), 'Management Accounting Practices and Techniques in Irish Manufacturing Firms', *paper presented at the 15th Annual Congress of the European Accounting Association, Madrid, Spain.*

Coates, J.B. and Longden, S.G. (1989), *Management Accounting: The Challenge of Technological Innovation,* London: Chartered Institute of Management Accountants.

Cooper R. (1988a), 'The rise of activity-based costing – Part Two: When do I need an activity-based cost system?', *Journal of Cost Management,* Fall, pp. 41–8.

Cooper, R. (1988b), 'The rise of activity-based costing – Part Three: How many cost drivers do you need, and how do you select them?', *Journal of Cost Management,* Winter, pp. 34–46.

Cooper, R. (1990a), 'Explicating the logic of ABC', *Management Accounting* (USA), November, pp. 58–60.

Cooper, R. (1990b), 'Cost classifications in unit-based and activity-based manufacturing cost systems', *Journal of Cost Management,* Fall, pp. 4–14.

Cooper, R. (1996), 'Costing techniques to support corporate strategy: evidence from Japan', *Management Accounting Research,* Vol. 7, No. 2, pp. 219–46.

Cooper, R. (1997), 'Activity-based costing: theory and practice', in Brinker, B.J. (ed.), *Handbook of Cost Management,* Warren, Gorham and Lamont, pp. B1–B33.

Cooper, R. and Kaplan, R.S. (1988), 'How cost accounting distorts product costs', *Management Accounting* (USA), April, pp. 20–7.

Cooper, R. and Kaplan, R.S. (1991), *The Design of Cost Management Systems: Text, Cases and Readings,* Englewood Cliffs, NJ: Prentice-Hall.

Cooper, R. and Kaplan, R.S. (1992), 'Activity based systems: measuring the costs of resource usage', *Accounting Horizons,* September, 1–13.

Drury, C. (1996), *Management and Cost Accounting,* London: International Thomson Business Press.

Drury, C., Braund, S., Osborne, P. and Tayles, M. (1993), *A Survey of Management Accounting Practices in UK Manufacturing Companies,* London: Chartered Association of Certified Accountants.

Drury, C. and Tayles, M. (1994), 'Product costing in UK manufacturing organisations', *European Accounting Review,* Vol. 3, No. 3, pp. 443–69.

Dugdale, D. and Jones, T.C. (1997), 'How many companies use ABC for stock valuation? A comment on Innes and Mitchell's questionnaire findings', *Management Accounting Research,* Vol. 8, No. 2, pp. 233–40.

Emore, J.R. and Ness, J.A. (1991), 'The slow pace of meaningful changes in cost systems', *Journal of Cost Management,* Winter, 1991, pp. 36–45.

Evans, H. and Ashworth, G. (1996), 'Survey conclusions: wake up to the competition', *Management Accounting,* May, 16–8.

Foster, G. and Swenson, D.W. (1997), 'Measuring the success of activity-based cost management and its determinants', *Journal of Management Accounting Research,* Vol. 9, pp. 109–42.

Friedman, A.L. and Lyne, S.R. (1995), *Activity-based Techniques: The Real Life Consequences,* London: Chartered Institute of Management Accountants.

Goetz, B. (1949), *Management Planning and Control: A Managerial Approach to Industrial Accounting,* New York: McGraw-Hill, p. 142.

Gosselin, M. (1997), 'The effect of strategy and organizational structure on the adoption and implementation of activity-based costing', *Accounting, Organizations and Society,* Vol. 22, No. 2, pp. 105–22.

Green, F.B. and Amenkhienan, F.E. (1992), 'Accounting innovations: a cross-sectional survey of manufacturing firms', *Journal of Cost Management,* Spring, pp. 58–64.

Hendricks, J.A. (1988), 'Applying cost accounting to factory automation', *Management Accounting* (USA), December, pp. 24–30.

Holzer, H.P. and Norreklit, H. (1991), 'Some thoughts on the cost accounting develop-ments in the United States', *Management Accounting Research,* March, pp. 3–13.

Hrisak, D. (1996), 'The controller as business strategist', *Management Accounting* (USA), December, 48–9.

Innes, J. and Mitchell, F. (1991), 'ABC: A survey of CIMA members', *Management Accounting*, October, 28–30.

Innes, J. and Mitchell, F. (1995), 'A survey of activity-based costing in the UK's largest companies', *Management Accounting Research,* June, pp. 137–54.

Johnson, H.T. and Kaplan, R.S. (1987), *Relevance Lost: The Rise and Fall of Management Accounting,* Harvard, Mass.: Harvard Business School Press.

Joshi, P.L. (1998), 'An explanatory study of activity-based costing practices and benefits in large-size manufacturing companies in India', *Accounting and Business Review,* Vol. 5, No. 1, pp. 65–93.

Joye, M.P. and Blayney, P.J. (1990), 'Cost and management accounting practice in Australian Manufacturing Companies: Survey Results', *Monograph No. 7,* University of Sydney.

Joye, M.P. and Blayney, P.J. (1991), 'Strategic Management Accounting Survey', *Monograph No. 8,* University of Sydney.

Kaplan, R.S. (1985), 'Accounting lag: the obsolescence of cost accounting systems', reprinted in Cooper, R. and Kaplan, R.S. (1991), *The Design of Cost Management Systems: Text, Cases and Readings,* Englewood Cliffs, NJ: Prentice-Hall, pp. 63–79.

Kaplan, R.S. (1988), 'One cost system isn't enough', *Harvard Business Review,* January/February, 61–6.

Kaplan, R.S. (1990), 'Contribution margin analysis: No longer relevant', *Journal of Management Accounting Research,* Fall, 2–15.

Kaplan, R.S. (1994), 'Management accounting (1984–1994): development of new practice and theory', *Management Accounting Research,* September and December, 247–60.

Kaplan, R.S. and Atkinson, A.A. (1998), *Advanced Management Accounting,* Englewood Cliffs, NJ: Prentice-Hall.

Kaplan, R.S. and Cooper, R. (1998), *Cost and Effect: Using Integrated Systems to Drive Profitability and Performance,* Harvard, Mass.: Harvard Business School Press.

Kerremans, M., Theunisse, H. and Van Overloop, G. (1991), 'The impact of automation and cost accounting', *Accounting and Business Research,* Spring, pp. 147–55.

Krumwiede, K.R. (1998), 'The implementation stages of activity-based costing and the impact of contextual and organizational factors', *Journal of Management Accounting Research,* Vol. 10, pp. 239–78.

Libby, T. and Waterhouse, J.H. (1996), 'Predicting change in management accounting systems', *Journal of Management Accounting Research,*Vol. 8, pp. 137–50.

Lukka, K. and Granlund, M. (1996), 'Cost accounting in Finland: current practice and trends of development', *European Accounting Review,* Vol. 5, No. 1, pp. 1–28.

Nicholls, B. (1992), 'ABC in the UK – a status report', *Management Accounting,* May, 22–3.

Porter, M. (1985), *Competitive Advantage: Creating and Sustaining Superior Performance,* New York: Free Press.

Shields, M.D. (1995), 'An empirical analysis of firms' implementation experiences with activity-based costing', *Journal of Management Accounting Research,* Vol. 7, pp. 148–66.

Shim, E. and Sudit, E. (1995), 'How manufacturers price products', *Management Accounting,* February, 37–9.

Simons, R. (1990), 'The role of management control systems in creating competitive advantage: new perspectives', *Accounting, Organizations and Society,* Vol. 15, No. 1/2, pp. 127–43.

Yoshikawa, T., Innes, J. and Mitchell, F. (1989), 'Japanese management accounting: a comparative survey', *Management Accounting,* November, 20–3.

Appendix I: Initial Questionnaire

Note
If this correspondence has been passed to you by a colleague could you please delete his or her address in the top left-hand corner and replace with your own name, company, job title and address.

(1) Please indicate below how frequently your organisation *routinely* analyses profits by the following categories:

	Monthly	Quarterly	Six-monthly	Annually	More than 1 year	Not routinely analysed
Products or services	☐ 1	☐ 2	☐ 3	☐ 4	☐ 5	☐ 6
Components	☐ 1	☐ 2	☐ 3	☐ 4	☐ 5	☐ 6
Customers or customer categories	☐ 1	☐ 2	☐ 3	☐ 4	☐ 5	☐ 6
Location (e.g. outlets, branches, regions and divisions)	☐ 1	☐ 2	☐ 3	☐ 4	☐ 5	☐ 6

(2) Please indicate below the *approximate* percentage of total sales revenue of your organisation that is accounted for by *external* sales of those products/services that are derived from using cost-plus pricing (whereby a percentage profit margin is added to the cost of providing the product/service to assist in setting the selling price).

0%	1–10%	11–20%	21–30%	31–40%	41–50%	Over 50%
☐ 1	☐ 2	☐ 3	☐ 4	☐ 5	☐ 6	☐ 7

(3) Please indicate whether your organisation accumulates costs for meeting financial accounting stock valuation requirements.

Yes ☐ No ☐

(4) Please tick one box below to provide an *approximate* indication of the turnover of your organisational unit.

£0–£25m	£26–£50m	£51–£75m	£76–£100m	£101–200m	£201–300m	Over £300m
☐ 1	☐ 2	☐ 3	☐ 4	☐ 5	☐ 6	☐ 7

(5) Please indicate the main business of your company or organisational unit.

Manufacturing	☐ 1	Retail	☐ 2	Service	☐ 3
Financial and commercial	☐ 4	Conglomerate	☐ 5	Other	☐ 6

(6) Is your company or group listed on any stock exchange? Yes ☐ No ☐

(7) Where are you located in the organisational structure?

☐ 1 at group head office ☐ 2 at divisional head office

☐ 3 at an operating unit ☐ 4 not applicable (no group structure)

(8) I am prepared to participate in the CIMA-sponsored research project. Yes ☐ No ☐

(9) If you are not prepared to participate in the project would you be kind enough to state the reason for your decision in the space below?

(10) If you have agreed to participate in the project can you please enter your telephone number here?

Appendix II: Questionnaire – Research into Cost System Design and Profitability Analysis

Section A - GENERAL QUESTIONS ABOUT YOUR PRODUCT / SERVICE ENVIRONMENT AND YOUR COSTING SYSTEM

Throughout the questionnaire tick one box per question unless indicated otherwise.

(A1) Which of the following most appropriately describes the products/services marketed by your organisation:

Customised products or services are marketed and costs are charged to each individual customer's order because each order is unique. ☐1

Output consists of a range of non-customised products or services resulting in sales normally consisting of many units of identical products/ services. ☐2

The products/services marketed consist of a combination of both the above categories. ☐3

Total output consists of a single product /service. ☐4

Other (please specify)..

....

(A2) The scale below relates to outputs of products or services ranging from (1) highly standardised to (7) totally customised. Please indicate the point on the scale which most appropriately describes the whole range of products or services marketed by your organisation.

Highly standardised 1	2	3	4	5	6	Totally Customised 7
☐	☐	☐	☐	☐	☐	☐

(A3) Please indicate whether your organisation traces costs to products, services or customers in order to value Work in Progress or Finished Stock for meeting financial accounting stock valuation and profit measurement requirements:

Costs are accumulated for stock valuation and their value is significant for financial reporting. ☐1

Costs are accumulated for stock valuation but their value is insignificant for financial reporting. ☐2

Costs are not accumulated for stock valuation requirements. *(Please omit questions A4 if you tick this box)* ☐3

(A4) Please indicate which of the following statements best describes the method of cost ascertainment in your organisation:

A single cost database is maintained from which appropriate cost information is extracted to provide the required information for both stock valuation and decision-making. ☐1

A separate cost database is maintained for stock valuation; cost information for decision-making is extracted from either other databases or other sources within my organisation. ☐2

Other (Please specify)..

....

(A5) Please indicate when the **last significant changes** were made in your costing system for generating information for decision-making.

Within last 12 months	1 -2 Years ago	2 -3 Years ago	3 – 4 Years ago	Over 4 Years ago
☐1	☐2	☐3	☐4	☐5

(A6) Please briefly describe any significant changes which have been made within the last 3 years.

....

....

....

(A7) Is your company **planning** to make **any significant changes** to the costing system within the next two years for generating information for decision-making?

Yes	No
☐1	☐2

(A8) If your company is planning any changes please briefly describe the nature of the proposed changes.

....

....

....

(A9) Please indicate on a scale of 1 to 7 the extent of competition for the major products/services of your organisation.

Low 1	2	3	4	5	6	Extremely Intensive 7
☐	☐	☐	☐	☐	☐	☐

(A10) How would you classify the market activities of your *competitors* during the past 5 years?

Becoming more predictable 1	2	3	4	5	6	Becoming less predictable 7
☐	☐	☐	☐	☐	☐	☐

(A11) During the past 5 years, the tastes and preferences of your *customers* have become:

Much easier to predict 1	2	3	4	5	6	Much harder to predict 7
☐	☐	☐	☐	☐	☐	☐

(A12) How intensive is each of the following in your industry?

a) Bidding for purchase of raw materials/supplies

Of negligible Intensity 1	2	3	4	5	6	Extremely Intensive 7
☐	☐	☐	☐	☐	☐	☐

b) Competition for manpower

Of negligible Intensity 1	2	3	4	5	6	Extremely Intensive 7
☐	☐	☐	☐	☐	☐	☐

c) Price competition

Of negligible Intensity 1	2	3	4	5	6	Extremely Intensive 7
☐	☐	☐	☐	☐	☐	☐

Section B - PROFITABILITY ANALYSIS AND DECISION-MAKING

This section relates only to cost information and profitability analysis routinely produced for decision-making (excluding cost information for setting selling prices). It does not apply to stock valuation where a separate database is maintained.

(B1) Please indicate below how frequently your organisation routinely analyses profits by the following categories:

	Monthly (1)	Quarterly (2)	Six monthly (3)	Annually (4)	More than one year (5)	Not routinely analysed (6)
Products or services	☐	☐	☐	☐	☐	☐
Components	☐	☐	☐	☐	☐	☐
Customers or customer categories	☐	☐	☐	☐	☐	☐
Location (eg. Outlets, branches, regions and divisions	☐	☐	☐	☐	☐	☐
Other (please specify below)						
....	☐	☐	☐	☐	☐	

For many of the questions within this section we use the general term 'cost object'. Please select one of the categories listed in Question B2 and relate all of your responses to those questions which use the term 'cost object' to the category that you have selected in Question B2. Ideally the category chosen should be the one which is regarded as the most important in your organisation for cost assignment and profitability analysis.

(B2) Please tick one box below to indicate your selected category for answering questions:

Products	Services	Components	Customers	Locations	Other(specify below)
□1	□2	□3	□4	□5	□6

....

....

....

(B3) For the category you selected in B2 above, over a typical year, how many different cost objects (different products, services, components, customers, locations) does your cost system assign costs to?

1-5	6-10	11-20	21-40	41-80	81-200	200-500.	Over 500
□1	□2	□3	□4	□5	□6	□7	□8

(B4) How important is the periodic profitability analysis in signalling the need to make key decisions relating to cost reduction, redesigning, outsourcing or discontinuing your chosen cost object.

Not important						Vitally Important
1	2	3	4	5	6	7
□	□	□	□	□	□	□

(B5) Please rank in order of importance the <u>three most important factors</u> (inserting in the boxes below 1 for the most important, 2 the next most important etc.) in signalling the need to make key decisions relating to cost reduction, redesigning, outsourcing or discontinuing your chosen cost object:

	Ranking
Past sales volume decline	□
Market share decline	□
Selling price decline	□
Predicted sales volume trend	□
Profitability analysis shows insufficient profit	□
Introduction of superior product by competitor	□

Other (please specify)

....

....

(B6) **For routine periodic profitability analysis** please specify whether or not the costs listed in (a) to (d) below are **traced to** your chosen cost object.

(a) **Direct incremental costs** that can be specifically traced to the cost object.

Costs **are traced** to the cost object ☐ 1

Costs **are not traced** to the cost object ☐ 2

(b) **Direct non - incremental costs** that can be directly traced to a specific cost object (examples of costs falling within this category would include depreciation of equipment specifically dedicated to a single product, service, customer category or location).

Costs **are traced** to the cost object ☐ 1

Costs **are not traced** to the cost object ☐ 2

Not applicable (costs within this category do not exist) ☐ 3

(c) **Indirect costs** where various allocation bases can be identified that are the causes of the costs varying in the long-term. Costs falling within this category are therefore assigned to cost objects **using allocation bases that are the causes of the cost**. (Examples of costs falling within this category include number of purchase orders for assigning the costs of purchasing activities, or number of transactions processed for assigning staff costs in a retail or financial services organisation).

Costs **are assigned** to the cost object ☐ 1

Costs are **not assigned** to the cost object ☐ 2

(d) **Indirect costs** where it is **not possible to identify allocation bases** that are the causes of the costs varying because costs tend to be fixed over a wide range of activity levels. Costs are therefore allocated using bases that are not the cause of the costs.(Examples of costs falling within this category are infrastructure costs such as costs relating to buildings, machinery and equipment which are used jointly by the cost object).

Costs **are allocated** to the cost object ☐ 1

Costs **are not allocated** to the cost object ☐ 2

(B7) For providing decision-making information, does your costing system **separately report** the categories of costs listed in Question B6.

(NB These categories of cost correspond to those given in Question B6, which should be consulted for any further clarification) (Tick one box for each line below)

		Yes(1)	No(2)
a)	**Direct incremental** costs are separately reported	☐	☐
b)	**Direct non-incremental** cost are separately reported	☐	☐
c)	**Indirect costs**, where allocation bases can be identified that are the causes of costs varying in the long term, are separately reported	☐	☐
d)	**Indirect costs,** where it is not possible to identify allocation bases that are the causes of costs varying because they tend to be fixed over a wide range of activity levels, are separately reported	☐	☐

(B8) When interpreting routinely generated profitability analysis information please tick one box to indicate which of the items listed below is the most important profitability measure for signalling the need to make cost reduction, discontinuation, redesign or outsourcing decisions relating to your chosen cost object. If you focus on more than one measure please also tick one box in column 2 to indicate the second most important measure.

	Most important measure (1)	Second most important measure (2)
(a) Revenues less direct variable (incremental) costs	☐	☐
(b) Revenues less direct variable (incremental) costs and direct fixed (non-incremental) costs	☐	☐
(c) Row (b) above less indirect costs that have been assigned to the cost object using cause and effect allocation bases, as described in Question B6 (item c)	☐	☐
(d) Row (c) above less those indirect costs where it is not possible to identify allocation bases that are the causes of the costs, as described in question B6 (item d)	☐	☐
(e) Bottom line net profit (sales less all costs)	☐	☐
(f) Not applicable (only one profitability measure is used)		☐
(g) None of the above (instead the measure or measures listed below are used)	☐	☐

If none of the measures listed above adequately explains which profitability measure is used by your organisation please list the measure (or measures) in the space provided below.

....

....

....

(B9) Which of the following best describe how profitability analysis is used for cost reduction, discontinuation, redesigning or outsourcing decisions.

Profitability analysis information is used directly for decision-making ☐1

Profitability analysis information represents attention-directing information for signalling the need for more detailed analysis to be undertaken. ☐2

(B10) Where profitability analysis is used as an attention-directing mechanism for signalling the need to undertake a more detailed appraisal, please briefly describe below the content of the information that is included in the appraisal.

....

....

....

(B11) Over a typical 1-year period please indicate below the percentage of items (proportion of business) within your chosen cost object that are discontinued because they have unsatisfactory profit expectations

Percentage of items discontinued

0-1	2-3	4-5	6-7	8-9	10-11	over 11
□1	□2	□3	□4	□5	□6	□7

(B12) For a typical 1-year period please indicate below the percentage of items (proportion of business) within your chosen cost object that is accounted for by the introduction of new products, services, components, customers or locations.

Percentage of products/components/services etc. introduced.

0-1	2-3	4-5	6-7	8-9	10-11	over 11
□1	□2	□3	□4	□5	□6	□7

(B13) Over a typical year please indicate (on a scale of 1 to 7) how frequently your organisation makes major redesign decisions and/or decides to move from internal to outside provision (i.e.outsourcing) of products (including components and processes) or services. (You should omit this question and tick N/A if you have not chosen products or services as your cost object).

never	rarely					Very frequently	N/A
1	2	3	4	5	6	7	8
□	□	□	□	□	□	□	□

(B14) The typical procedure for assigning indirect costs to cost objects involves a 2-stage process. In the first stage overheads are allocated to cost centres (cost pools). In the second stage overhead allocation rates (or cost driver rates) are established for each cost centre to assign overheads to cost objects. **Please indicate below approximately how many separate cost centres (cost pools) are used to assign overheads to your chosen cost object.** (For example, if your organisation has 5 cost centres all of which use a single allocation rate (such as direct labour hours) please tick 5 in the box below to indicate that 5 separate cost centres have been established).

Number of cost centres (cost pools) which have their own overhead allocation (charge out) rate

1	2-3	4-5	6-10	11-20	21-30	31- 50	Over 50
□1	□2	□3	□4	□5	□6	□7	□8

(B15) **Please indicate below how many separate (different) overhead allocation recovery methods (cost drivers) are used in the second stage of the two-stage procedure described in Question B14.** (For example, if your organisation has five separate cost centres all using direct labour hours as the overhead recovery method, then please tick the first box to indicate that a single method is used. Alternatively, if your organisation has 5 cost centres and uses two methods of overhead recovery allocation bases (such as direct labour hours and machine hours) you should tick 2 in the box below.

Number of separate overhead recovery methods (cost drivers) used

1	2	3	4	5	6	7-10	Over 10
□1	□2	□3	□4	□5	□6	□7	□8

(B16) For the overhead allocation recovery methods / cost drivers that you have identified in question B15 above please list below (up to a maximum of 6) which are the most important in your organisation.

....

....

....

....

(B17) Are infrastructure costs (such as depreciation, property costs, lighting and heating of the factory or administrative facilities) charged to cost centres and included within the overhead allocation rates that are charged to your chosen cost object?

Yes	No
□1	□2

Other (please specify) ....

(B18) If you have answered YES to Question B17 please indicate if infrastructure costs are categorised separately when extracting information for making cost reduction, discontinuation, redesign or outsourcing decisions.

Yes	No
□1	□2

(B19) Please indicate on a scale of (1) to (7) how <u>accurate</u> you think your cost system is in assigning overheads to your chosen cost object for the purpose of making cost reduction, discontinuation, redesign or outsourcing decisions. (Please tick box 8 which refers to not applicable if overheads are not assigned to your chosen cost object).

Not very accurate						Extremely accurate	N/A
1	2	3	4	5	6	7	8
□	□	□	□	□	□	□	□

(B20) How <u>satisfied</u> are you with the accuracy of your cost system in assigning overheads to your chosen cost object for the purpose of making cost reduction, discontinuation, redesign or outsourcing decisions. (Please tick box 8 which refers to not applicable if overheads are not assigned to your chosen cost object).

not at all satisfied						Extremely satisfied	N/A
1	2	3	4	5	6	7	8
□	□	□	□	□	□	□	□

(B21) Has your organisation implemented Activity-based Costing (ABC)?

Yes	No
□1	□2

(B22) If you answered yes to Question B21, please tick the appropriate boxes below to indicate how ABC is used in your organisation.

ABC has been implemented and it is used to assign costs to cost objects for decision-making. □$_1$

ABC has been implemented and it is used to cost activities for cost management purposes (Eg. to prioritise those activities that need to be studied closely for the purpose of cost reduction). □$_2$

Activity analysis is undertaken but the activities are not costed □$_3$

Other (please specify)..

....

(B23) **Please indicate on a scale of 1 to 7 how much variation you think there is in the consumption of support department overheads by the different items within your chosen cost object.** Support departments are defined as those departments that provide essential services to support the provision of your chosen cost object. Hence their costs cannot be directly traced to cost objects. Examples of support departments include maintenance, production engineering and scheduling in manufacturing organisations and data processing departments in non-manufacturing organisations.

Little variation						Considerable Variation
1	2	3	4	5	6	7
□	□	□	□	□	□	□

(B24) What proportion of total sales <u>volume</u> is accounted for by the top 20% of the best selling items within your chosen cost object (products, services customers)? For example, if your organisation has 100 products, services, or customers, what percentage of total sales volume is accounted for by the top 20 best selling items.

20-30%	31-40%	41-50%	51-60%	61-70%	71-80%	Over 80%
□$_1$	□$_2$	□$_3$	□$_4$	□$_5$	□$_6$	□$_7$

(B25) What proportion of total sales <u>volume</u> is accounted for by the bottom 20% of the lowest selling items within your chosen cost object (products, services or customers)?

1-3%	4-6%	7-9%	10-12%	13-15%	16-18%	Over 18%
□$_1$	□$_2$	□$_3$	□$_4$	□$_5$	□$_6$	□$_7$

(B26) For your chosen cost object please indicate on the scale below how much variation there is in the sales <u>volume</u> between the top 20% of the best selling items and the bottom 20% of the lowest selling items.

Little variation						Considerable Variation
1	2	3	4	5	6	7
□	□	□	□	□	□	□

(B27) For your organisation please provide an approximate percentage breakdown of your cost structure by entering the percentages in the appropriate spaces below:

Manufacturing Organisations	%
Materials that can be directly traced to your chosen cost object	
(e.g. Products/Customers)	
Labour that can be directly traced to the cost object	
Non-manufacturing costs that can be directly traced to the cost object	
Production overhead that **cannot** be directly traced to the cost object	
Non-manufacturing overhead that **cannot** be traced to the cost object	___
	100

Non-Manufacturing Organisations	%
Costs that can be directly traced to your chosen object	
(e.g. services, locations or customers)	
Costs that cannot be directly traced to the cost object	___
	100

Questions B28-B31 are concerned with product, service or customer profitability analysis. If your chosen cost object is not one of these categories please omit these questions and proceed to Section C.

(B28) Please indicate (for your chosen cost object) which of the following statements best describes the classification of products, services or customers of your organisation:

Individual products, services or customers are not classified by product lines or categories(if you tick this box please proceed to Section C) ☐1

Individual products, services or customers are grouped together and treated as lines of similar products/services (or similar customer categories). ☐2

(B29) Which of the following best reflects the reporting system of your organisation:

Profits are analysed by product/service lines or customer categories and not by individual products/services or customers within the product line or customer category. (If you tick this box please answer Question B30 and then proceed to Section C). ☐1

Profits are analysed by *individual* products/services or customers within each product/service line or customer category. (If you tick this box please proceed to Question B31) ☐2

(B30) If your periodic profitability analysis reports analyse profits by product/service lines or customer categories but not by *individual* products, services or customers please indicate which of the following statements is correct:

Even though the profitability of *individual* products, services or customers is not routinely reported; individual product, service or customer costs can be extracted from the database when the need arises. ☐1

The costing system does not accumulate costs by *individual* products, services or customers and therefore it is not possible to ascertain their profitability. ☐2

(B31) Where profits are analysed by *individual* products, services or customers please indicate below how those joint costs which can be directly traced to a product/service line or customer category, but **not** to the *individual* products, services or customers are recorded in the profitability analysis. (Examples of such costs include advertising relating to the *whole* product line or customer category but not to *individual* products or customers within the line).

Joint costs are not allocated to individual products, services or customers but are directly charged as a lump sum against the aggregate contributions arising from all of the items within the product/service line or customer category. ☐1

Joint costs are allocated to the individual items within a product/service line or customer category. ☐2

Other (please specify) ....

....

Section C - COST ACCUMULATION FOR STOCK VALUATION

You should omit this section completely if you have indicated in question A3 that your organisation does not trace costs to products/services for stock valuation.

(C1) Please indicate below the value of stocks as an approximate percentage of annual sales turnover for your organisation.

Value of stocks as a percentage of sales turnover

0-4	5-9	10-14	15-19	20-24	25-29	30% and over
☐1	☐2	☐3	☐4	☐5	☐6	☐7

(C2) Does your organisation use an activity-based costing system to trace costs to products/components/ services for stock valuation.

Yes	No
☐1	☐2

(C3) Please indicate on a scale of (1) to (7) how <u>accurate</u> you think your cost system is in assigning overheads for the purpose of stock valuation.

Not very accurate						Extremely accurate
1	2	3	4	5	6	7
☐	☐	☐	☐	☐	☐	☐

(C4) How <u>satisfied</u> are you on a scale of (1) to (7) with the accuracy of your cost system in assigning overheads for the purpose of stock valuation.

Not at all satisfied 1	2	3	4	5	6	Extremely satisfied 7
☐	☐	☐	☐	☐	☐	☐

Questions C6-C8 below are a repeat of Questions B14-B16. If you have indicated in question A4 that the same database is used to extract cost information for both decision-making and stock valuation requirements, and your responses to questions B14-B16 also describe your organisation's costing system for stock valuation, please tick the appropriate box in Question C5 below and proceed to section D.

(C5) Please clarify the cost accumulation system which is used for stock valuation.

The responses to questions B14-B16 correctly describe the cost accumulation system for stock valuation. ☐1

The responses to Questions B14-B16 **do not** correctly describe the cost accumulation system for stock valuation ☐2
(If you tick this response please complete Questions C6-C8)

Other (*please specify*)..

(C6) For stock valuation please indicate below approximately how many separate cost centres (cost pools) are used in your organisation (*Please refer back to Question B14 for guidance on the terms used in this question.*)

Number of cost centres (cost pools) which have their own overhead allocation (charge out) rate

1	2-3	4-5	6-10	11-20	21-30	31-50	Over 50
☐1	☐2	☐3	☐4	☐5	☐6	☐7	☐8

(C7) Please indicate below how many separate overhead allocation recovery methods (cost drivers) are used for stock valuation in your organisation. (*Please refer back to question B15 for guidance on the terms used in this question.*)

Number of separate overhead recovery methods /cost drivers used

1	2	3	4	5	6	7-10	Over 10
☐	☐	☐	☐	☐	☐	☐	☐

(C8) Please list below (up to a maximum of 6) the most important overhead allocation recovery methods/cost drivers that are used for stock valuation.

....

....

....

....

Section D - COST INFORMATION FOR SETTING SELLING PRICES

This section relates only to cost information for cost-plus pricing (whereby a percentage profit margin is added to the costs of providing the product or service to assist in setting selling prices). In some organisations established selling prices will exist and a firm will have little or no influence on the prices of products or services. If cost-plus pricing is not used in your organisation please tick the appropriate box in question D1 and proceed to section E. However, if cost-plus pricing is sometimes used will you please complete section D and relate your responses only to cost accumulation for this purpose.

(D1) For sales to **external** customers, is cost-plus pricing sometimes used to assist in setting selling prices?

cost-plus pricing is sometimes used ☐1

cost-plus pricing is **not** used ☐2
(If you have ticked this response please omit the remaining questions in this section and proceed to section E)

(D2) Using a scale of 1 to 7, please tick a box below to indicate how important the derived cost-plus selling price is in determining the final selling price.

Of little importance 1	2	3	4	5	6	Of vital importance 7
☐	☐	☐	☐	☐	☐	☐

(D3) Approximately what percentage of total sales revenue of your organisation is accounted for by **external sales** of those products /services that are derived from using cost-plus pricing?

0-10%	11-20%	21-30%	31-40%	41-50%	51-70%	over70%
☐1	☐2	☐3	☐4	☐5	☐6	☐7

(D4) Does your organisation use an activity-based costing system for computing costs to derive cost-plus selling prices?

Yes	No
☐1	☐2

(D5) Please indicate on a scale of (1) to (7) how <u>accurate</u> you think your cost system is in assigning overheads for determining selling prices. (If overheads are not assigned for cost plus pricing please tick box 8).

Not very accurate 1	2	3	4	5	6	Extremely accurate 7	N/A 8
☐	☐	☐	☐	☐	☐	☐	☐

(D6) How <u>satisfied</u> are you with the accuracy of your cost system in assigning overheads for determining selling prices. (If overheads are not assigned for cost plus pricing please tick box 8).

Not at all satisfied 1	2	3	4	5	6	Extremely satisfied 7	N/A 8
☐	☐	☐	☐	☐	☐	☐	☐

(D7) Please indicate whether or not the costs listed in (a) to (d) below are traced to cost objects (i.e. specific products, services or customers) for cost-plus pricing.

(a) Direct incremental costs that can be specifically traced to the cost object.

Costs are traced to the cost object ☐1

Costs are not traced to the cost object ☐2

(b) Direct non - incremental costs that can be directly traced to a specific product or service (examples of costs falling within this category would include depreciation of equipment specifically dedicated to a single product, service, customer category).

Costs are traced to the cost object ☐1

Costs are not traced to the cost object ☐2

Not applicable (costs within this category do not exist) ☐3

(c) Those indirect costs where various allocation bases can be identified that are the causes of the cost varying in the long term. Costs falling within this category are therefore assigned to cost objects using allocation bases that are the causes of the cost. (Examples of costs falling within this category include number of purchase orders for assigning the costs of purchasing activities, or number of transactions processed for assigning staff costs in a retail or financial services organisation).

Costs are assigned to the cost object ☐1

Costs are not assigned to the cost object ☐2

(d) Indirect costs where it is not possible to identify allocation bases that are the causes of the costs varying because costs tend to be fixed over a wide range of activity levels. Costs are therefore allocated using allocation bases that are not the cause of the costs. (Examples of costs falling within this category are infrastructure costs such as costs related to buildings, machinery and equipment which are used jointly by the cost object).

Costs are allocated to the cost object ☐1

Costs are not allocated to the cost object ☐2

Questions D9-D11 below are a repeat of Questions B14-B16. If you have indicated in question A4 that the same database is used to extract cost information for both routine decision-making and stock valuation requirements, and if your responses to Questions B14-B16 also describe your organisation's costing system for accumulating product/service costs for cost-plus pricing, please tick the appropriate box (or boxes) in question D8 below and proceed to Section E.

(D8) Please clarify the cost accumulation system which is used to assist in setting selling prices.

(a) The responses to Questions B14-B16 correctly describe the costing system for accumulating product/service costs for cost-plus pricing. ☐$_1$

(b) The database for stock valuation (C6-C8) correctly describes the costing system for accumulating product /service costs for cost-plus pricing. ☐$_2$

(c) The responses to Questions B14-B16 **do not** correctly describe the costing system for accumulating product/service costs for cost-plus pricing. (*If you tick this response please complete questions D9-D11*) ☐$_3$

(d) Other (*please specify*)..

....

(D9) For accumulating product/service costs for cost-plus pricing please indicate below approximately how many cost centres (cost pools) are used in your organisation. *(Please refer back to Question B14 for guidance on the terms used in this question)*

Number of cost centres (cost pools) which have their own overhead allocation (charge out) rate

1	2-3	4-5	6-10	11-20	21-30	31-50	Over 50
☐$_1$	☐$_2$	☐$_3$	☐$_4$	☐$_5$	☐$_6$	☐$_7$	☐$_8$

(D10) Please indicate below how many separate overhead allocation recovery methods (cost drivers) are used for accumulating product/service costs for cost plus pricing. *(Please refer back to question B15 for guidance on the terms used in this question)*

Number of separate overhead recovery methods/(cost drivers) used.

1	2	3	4	5	6	7-10	Over10
☐$_1$	☐$_2$	☐$_3$	☐$_4$	☐$_5$	☐$_6$	☐$_7$	☐$_8$

(D11) Please list below (up to a maximum of 6) the most important overhead allocation methods (cost drivers) that are used for accumulating product service costs for determining selling prices.

....

....

....

....

Section E DEFINING ACTIVITY LEVELS IN COST ASSIGNMENT

(E1) The second stage of the two-stage overhead procedure described in Question B14 requires that for each cost centre (cost pool) overhead absorption (cost driver) rates are established by dividing cost centre overheads by the level of activity for the allocation base (cost driver). Alternatively, the second stage can be implemented by allocating cost centre overheads to cost objects based on their proportionate usage of the allocation base. Both approaches require a measure of the activity for the allocation base (cost driver).

Please tick one of the boxes below which most appropriately describes how the activity level is determined:

Budgeted or estimated annual activity □1

Maximum practical annual capacity that is available
(this is the capacity that is expected to be available
for the period and includes both utilised and unutilised capacity). □2

Estimated average long-run activity derived from expected activity
over several years (e.g. 3-5 years) □3

Not applicable (overheads are not assigned to the cost object) □4

Other (please specify)... □5

....

(E2) Does your business unit measure the cost of unutilised capacity for cost centres/cost pools)

Yes	No
□1	□2

(E3) If you have answered Yes to the above question then please briefly describe in the space below how the cost of unutilised capacity is determined.

....

....

....

....

Section F - QUESTIONS RELATING TO YOUR OWN COMPANY OR ORGANISATIONAL UNIT

(F1) Please tick the box below which best describes your organisation.

My company or organisational unit is part of a group structure. □1

My company or organisational unit is **not** part of a group structure. □2

(F2) Is your company or group listed on any stock exchange? Yes □1 No □2

Questions F3 to F5 relate to the reporting unit of which you are an employee.

(F3) Please briefly describe the industry sector / type of business to which your organisational unit belongs.

....

....

(F4) Please indicate the main business of your company or organisational unit.

Manufacturing	□1	Retail	□2	Service	□3
Financial and commercial	□4	Conglomerate	□5	Other	□6

(F5) Please indicate the turnover of your company or organisational unit.

£0-£25m	£26m-£50m	£51m-£75m	£76m-£100m	£101m-£200m	£201m-£300m	Over £300m
□1	□2	□3	□4	□5	□6	□7

Question F6 and F7 relate to the Group of which your reporting unit is a part.
Please omit these questions if your reporting unit is not part of a group structure.

(F6) Please indicate the sales revenue of your organisational unit as a percentage of total group turnover

0-5%	6-10%	11-20%	21-30%	31-40%	41-50%	Over 50%
□1	□2	□3	□4	□5	□6	□7

(F7) Is the head office in: the United Kingdom □1 or overseas □2

Section G - QUESTIONS ABOUT YOURSELF

Would you please provide us with the following information which will only be used to contact you directly in the event of a query about your responses and to send you a summary report of our findings. It will not be revealed to third parties.

Person completing the questionnaire:

Name .... Job Title ....

Organisation/Company Name ....

Address ....

.... Telephone No ....

(G1) Where are you located in the organisational structure?

☐1 at group head office ☐2 at divisional head office

☐3 at an operating unit ☐4 not applicable, no group structure

(G2) Please indicate the length of time since you qualified as an accountant.

☐1 2 years ☐2 2-5 years ☐3 5-10 years ☐4 Over 10 years

(G3) Would it be possible for a meeting to be arranged to discuss some of the issues raised by this questionnaire?

Meeting possible ☐1 Meeting not possible ☐2

(G4) Please indicate on a scale of 1 to 7 how interested you would be in attending a seminar presented by ourselves that describes and discusses the results of this research.

Not interested 1	2	3	4	5	6	Very interested 7
☐	☐	☐	☐	☐	☐	☐

Thank you for taking the time to complete the questionnaire. We would welcome any further comments you may have, please use space on the questionnaire for this.

Now will you please return it in the prepaid envelope we have supplied. If you have any questions please do not hesitate to contact one of us.

Professor Colin Drury
University of Huddersfield
Tel: 01484 472299 (direct line)
01484 472840 (secretary)

E-mail j.c.drury@hud.ac.uk

Mike Tayles
University of Bradford Management Centre
Tel: 01274 234403 (direct line)
01274 234344 (secretary)

E-mail m.e.tayles@bradford.ac.uk

Appendix III: Respondents' Comments on Question B10 of Appendix II

- Economic viability of the assets – future production, prices, tax reserves (oil/gas). Strategic value of the asset – synergy with other assets in the portfolio.
- Focus on high-value internal process costs and on recharges in from other group businesses.
- All relevant information that can be obtained/provided with variance analysis in both qualitive and quantitative terms.
- With a high level of fixed costs, reduced profitability tends to be the result of: selling price too low, direct costs too high, additional services not recovered – these areas are examined.
- Performance gap analysis – using externally benchmarked rates.
- Income generated by research project of contract less direct costs (e.g. subcontract work, travel) to arrive at a level of contribution.
- Net worth of product (i.e. B8 1B) – short-term, long-term view of product sales volume, alternative product.
- Analysis of contracts of certain types or for certain customers.
- Full supply chain costing, i.e. revenue less distribution less production. (In most internal base measures distribution is less detailed.)
- A marginal cost analysis using all directly related costs where available, including indirect costs which can be linked to product by cause.
- Impact of decision on other products sold in the same market, overall impact on fixed cost recoveries, strategic importance of market segment.
- Comparison of market share, revenue trends and manufacturing costs/methods will determine future policy.
- Product life cycle status, market trends, product strategy. Future: activity analysis of commercial/logistics costs.
- Mainly future plans and budgets and alternative uses for the staff.
- Contribution per plant hour, DCF calculations, payback, risk analysis.
- Under-utilisation of plant, fixed asset write-offs, non-absorbed product-related costs, number of customers, alternative products for existing customers, environmental issues.
- Sales price and volume are of primary importance.

- Cost allocation bases are reviewed – standard. Actual analysis confirms assessment made on the basis of more appropriate marginal issues and non-financial issues, including indirects not in costing system.
- Variable costs will be used as reported by the costing system. The other costs all have an 'allocation'-based nature and therefore when, for example, reviewing saving or outsourcing we attempt to review the best scenario of actual cost or actual costs saved.
- Depends on the strategy of the business. Typically, this *may* include projected volume, market analysis, competitor costs, customer value analysis, etc.
- It is the starting point/catalyst for reviewing future plans.
- Impact on co-products and by-products.
- For example, volume effect on product cost.
- Profitability by category, signalling the need for more detailed information by product. Historical profitability comparisons.
- More detailed analysis of the item(s) causing concern produced as a matter of course.
- Gross margins not at acceptable level, therefore: gross margins, standard product costs by nature of expense and by process, technical standards.
- Profitability by cells is quite a broad-brush indicator – we would start to look at individual customers or product ranges within the cell if a problem was highlighted.
- Return on capital employed, customer profile.
- Comparisons between plants (internal benchmarking), comparisons with targets and prior years.
- Product profitability – revenue less standard cost.
- All relevant information.
- Sales revenue less materials and labour.
- A detailed analysis of how the product is made is undertaken, trying to distinguish the non-value-added activities, then try to reduce the non-value-added times down.
- Full sales analysis margin, manufacturing loss analysis, marketing analysis.
- Cost-driven analysis, cost of change product re-engineering, pricing decisions over approach to account profitability, etc.
- Analysis is based on annual standard cost, appraisal checks, actual costs and standard hour recovery base.
- Revenue, gross margin, selling and general expenses, absolute and percentage revenue, also all compared with plan and prior year.
- Profitability (contribution) of product, profitability of group of products sold to customers(s), competitive threat – strategic pricing.
- If a sub-business unit shows a poor profit performance, a forecast of future profit performance is prepared before any decisions are made.
- Future predicted sales volumes and prices, level of competition, cost of re-engineering.
- Market trends, technological advances, competitor activity.
- Direct material analysis, direct labour cycle times, variable overhead (consumables) analysis.

- Competitor data, market forecasts.
- Profitability by customer.
- Usually to verify the assumptions of bills of material and process route. Significant indirect non-incremental costs.
- Alternative processing, quality of service, risk to performance.
- Market prospects for other future work, cost of retaining workforce, alternative markets/products.
- Mainly engineering verifying/improving the physical information to make a product cost, e.g. times, materials.
- Man-hour charging rates.
- Gross profit is continually analysed to show non-profit-making items.
- Cost/benefit of improvements to manufacturing process/re-engineering, technical specification (indicating need for engineering development), market competitiveness (price, performance, volume).
- Analysis of the standard bills of materials.
- We would consider verifying the accuracy of any cost allocations, any new replacement product on the horizon, expected market size, market share.
- Product and product group (segment) marginal costing.
- Before making a decision to discontinue a product, its relationship with other products within the product portfolio must be identified and the effect of discontinuing the product analysed.
- The associated overheads/forced costs and whether these can be reduced or else recovered by a more profitable product being made using the freed capacity.
- Cost of alternative sourced materials/in-market pricing opportunities/group internal pricing decisions.
- Check on costs and net sales revenues received and total margin with customer, etc.
- Detailed causal analysis of major contributors to profitability and options; alternatives in meeting the objectives.
- Non-financials, e.g. importance of individual product to range offering, importance of customer/competitor position. Review of marginal cost benefits.
- Numbers of customers serviced, delivery information, calls made.
- Any re-engineering of the product primarily impacts on material costs. However, any detailed appraisal would also look more closely at 'direct non-incremental' costs and actual delivery costs for that cost object.
- More analysis on the indirect cost drivers is held 'off line' from the main system in a separate database.
- Review of product components, review of direct customer costs, review of site overhead levels.
- PC-driven – start with current base cost and then show what incremental savings would be made each time a specific action is undertaken.
- Shareholder value, return on assets, cash flow.
- Gross profitability analysis appraised in terms of variances due to price, volume, mix and specific cost of sales movements (largely foreign exchange-related in terms of manufacturing unit currency).

- Customer- and product-specific detail, with as much specific costs that are known replacing previous apportionments.
- Varies by situation, impossible to briefly describe a 'for instance'.
- Consumer/customer research, re-engineering options, promotional/pricing, contracting options.
- Sales volumes, material costs, stocks of finished goods, gross margin.
- Margin at product level – decide whether to rationalise based on production yield variance from standard and effect of currency deviations in foreign markets.
- Raw material price, production volume, machine efficiency, production speed, production route, bills of materials.
- Sales/market trends, customer base, 'commercial considerations'.
- The appraisal is based on a simple ABC model using an Excel spreadsheet.
- Disposal costs, IRR calculation of impact.
- Would bring in overheads at this stage.
- Competitor activity/positioning or repositioning product in market/forecast volumes/mix of product to be sold.
- More detailed analysis of direct and relevant costs.
- Checking the information is sound and abnormal events/costs.
- Market share analysis; marginal cost analysis; historical sales volumes; prices; future cost trend analysis.
- Future sales forecast, future direct cost forecast, future specific fixed overhead forecast. Opportunities and threats both in the market place and in manufacturing.
- Total contract revenues and costs over a representative period – usually twelve months.
- Customers, spread of distribution, inter-branch manufacturing, level of central costs allocated, personnel review.
- Market intelligence re future demand volumes.
- Net cash flows of all the aspects of the decision area, e.g. discontinued stock sales, stock rebuild, relay of stores, etc.
- Availability of alternative product – estimates of that product's profit.
- Varies depending on the object of the decision – e.g. can be 'political' such as 'loss leaders'.
- High-level route profitability analysis, plus benchmarking against other routes – including by cost element.
- Predicted sales volumes, costs, charges, inflation, market share, elasticity of demand.
- Total network impact (may include sister company in group).
- Degree of fixed avoidable costs, marginal cost elements, volumes involved, impact on other products.
- Comparison of key elements to target standards set.
- Profitability analysis as above, forecasts, sensitivity analysis.
- Project team set up for area of concern.
- £s, full time equivalents, process volumes, unit costs – by division for each product process.

- Sales margin analysis. Other income-generation opportunities.
- Repricing or new product launch has a direct effect on sales/holdings of existing range. Marginal cash-flow analysis is used to evaluate proposed changes to the product range.
- Competitor ratios/prior year data/strategic five-year and operational current-year data.
- An annual review of the product portfolio is carried out. Business cases are prepared for product upgrade or where poor performance necessitates a review of the product.
- Incremental profitability is the attention-director, and then a product is fully costed in the overall analysis.
- Resource utilisation (i.e. people) across the business may affect interpretation of 'standard' costs/margins; + (subjective) view of level of indirect costs; + level of risk.
- Customer profitability, profit by sales representative or sales channel, profit by customer type/industry.
- Sales less standard costs, warranty costs, rework costs, price variances, labour variances.
- Current project estimate at completion.
- Review is carried out from a marketing, sales and finance perspective.
- Work content time, material content, other direct costs.
- Cash flows – people issues – management, spans of control, quality of staff, competition.
- Product – potential for re-engineering. Location – potential for restructure.
- Market penetration. Product succession. Market demand.
- Effect on overhead recovery in the factories. Effect on the rest of the business with the customer.
- Commercial issues. Divisional/customer analysis/market place.
- Market consideration. Strategic considerations – competitors, etc.